Dear You,

Live!

Love,

Life

Awaking your spirit, overcoming fears & excuses, and living a purposeful, fulfilling life.

"Toto, I have a feeling we're not in Kansas anymore."

~ L. Frank Baum

Let's do this.

"If I read one more 'you can do it, rah, rah, rah, don't give up' book I'll be sick." Sound familiar? Of course we know we can "do it." But we often ignore opportunities and challenges because they require change and effort. Of course, we're also missing the accompanying lessons. If we had to pass periodic life lesson tests we'd pay better attention.

So, here we are. How you got here is important–after all, it's your life. From here, you'll build on your experiences and discover how living a compelling, rich life is a freeing, exhilarating time of times. Your biographer will earn their pay, writing a riveting account of a life abundantly lived. One replayed over and again in the reader's imagination.

If you need a little push to get started, here's a sobering fact: The end of the world comes to more than 153,000 people each and every day. When your day comes, and it will, leave more than a grainy newspaper photo, eight digits, and a hyphen as your legacy. Make a commitment to squeeze every ounce of life from your gift of life. Get off your ass. Effort provides a singular advantage. *You're doing something.* Don't simply attend school, get a ~~job~~ career, then spend the rest of your life lamenting and groaning about it. Fill in the blanks.

Dying, leaving only a date of birth and death as your obituary, cheats everyone. Mostly you. Those dying without a white-knuckle life story shortchange themselves and leave loved ones wondering, "what if?" A simple existence can be rewarding. Simply existing? Not so much.

Make the conscious choice to be remembered without the hyphens and without the digits. To be remembered through your living days with dates simply as a footnote. That's your yardstick.

Any person believing they are immortal need only to spend a quiet morning walking through a cemetery. We live staring at the eyes of death. Every breath, every blink of an eye, every twitch. Each step one step closer to our inevitable destination. When the last ticket is punched, the earthly destination is the same for all of us. It's the journey–the adventure–that is unique for each of us. Seeing life as a path to death shouldn't speed the process of living, but drunken it with possibilities. If you choose not to partake, then you do not cheat death. You cheat life.

Whenever I read bios of long-passed people I admire, I check the dates of their birth and death to get some perspective into their environment, the social ways of the times, the general thinking, and accepted norms. That is quickly followed by counting on my fingers, doing the mental math, and having a "holy bejeezus" moment with the realization of what so many of these greats accomplished in such relatively (by today's life expectancies) small amounts of time. I better get busy. We *all* better get busy. Birth through death: A–Z, but just look at the unlimited game of Life Scrabble you can play with B through Y.

You're not going to solve all the world's ills. That's not your job anyway. You should, however, do something every day that creates a beneficial difference in your life. So, about that bucket list. Yes, you should have one. But to this, I add, "die with dreams." Without dreams, you've already stopped living. Don't settle for just a bucket list. Make a ginormous helibucket size list. If you manage to empty that, fly low, scoop up another bucketful of dreams and reimagine your thirst for life.

As writers go, you'll quickly discover that I'm a sprinter not a marathoner. As Friedrich Nietzsche said, "It is my ambition to say in ten sentences what others say in a whole book." Subjects are tackled with brevity. The goal is to lasso the topic, wrestle it onto the page, then set it free for your imagination and consideration. To make you think. A reminder to get off your rear and live your adventure. No one can do that for you. Start living. Starting now. Be your own diversion.

You're on the clock.

Let's start by taking a look at the principal obstacles keeping you from reaching your goals, and tackling how to overcome them. We begin building by laying this foundational tenet: *If you are going to doubt something, doubt your limits.*

So then, what are the common reasons and excuses for not living your desired life?

Not Knowing What You Want

Ask most people what they want in life and you'll get general answers and ideas. This is because the mind works on the principle of least effort. For instance, if I tell myself, "I want to make more money," and I pick a quarter up off the ground, my mind may believe it has accomplished its goal.

You must create an image of what you want and set a mental strategy to achieve it. Here's an example: You call a travel agent and tell them that you want a perfect vacation, stating, "Not St. Louis." Since your travel agent doesn't have any idea of what your perfect vacation is, the only thing they can think of is, of course, St. Louis. It's possible that you may wind up in Tulsa, OK (not that Tulsa is an undesirable destination). If you were to request a destination comprised of "85 degrees, balmy, palm trees, ocean breeze, resort with 24/7 room service," you'd get a different result.

Take some time and make a list your "musts." Make a list of desires. A list of important people and things. Things you must do. Things you'd love to do. Places to see. You get the idea. If you don't know where you are going, any road will take you there. And, unfortunately, just as water follows the path of least resistance, so often do we. The good news is that you have control. Setting sail without a compass or rudder is like throwing yourself in the surf expecting to stop the ocean. The message: *Create a defined image of what you want.*

Not Being Mentally, Spiritually, and Emotionally Aligned
Let's use money as an example all of us can relate to. Following, are a few beliefs that people have about money:

- It's wonderful and people with gobs of money lead wonderful lives.
- Money is evil and people with gobs of money do bad things to people and the planet.
- People with money are incredibly happy.
- People with money are users.
- People with no money are bums, deadbeats, and losers.

When it comes to money, a person can hold all these (and other) beliefs simultaneously. Yet even if someone has only two of these–say for example, "money is good *and* people with money do terrible things"–it leads to inner-conflict. These contradictory beliefs create a mental incongruence that leads to self-sabotage about what to accomplish with money. In the background, the mind is simply trying to resolve the conflict: "Am I supposed to go after money because it's good or should I avoid it?" In this instance, the mind has to reach a compromise of how much money is okay and how much it feels is deserved.

Here are two examples:

- A structural engineer is asked for a proposal to design a bridge. Internally though, she hasn't reached a decision on whether this bridge would be the best solution. Part of her is thinking that a ferry terminal and boat system would be more cost effective and utilitarian. Perhaps the bridge shouldn't be built at all. Bottom line? Nothing of consequence happens till she reaches an inner—consensus. Until then, enjoy your swim.

- Let's say you need to make forty calls a day to achieve your sales goals, yet for whatever reason, you never seem to make forty calls a day. I'll bet you can rationalize it. Minds work overtime to continually justify behavior that results from subconscious conflicts (kids take too much of your time, school, errands, favorite TV show, neighbors, et al). *Yet there are people in similar situations that make those forty calls. How?* They are professionally, personally, and spiritually aligned to achieve the goal. It is not a *question* of "why can't I do it?" It is an *answer* of "how I did it."

Bottom line, you get what you believe you deserve, and it applies to everything you want. You have to be 100% aligned.

Not Having a Mental Strategy

Accomplishment creates good feelings. Let's focus on the above sales call example for a moment. If you believe that your next call will result in rejection, then you will feel rejected before you make the call. It's self-fulfilling. Of course, if you make the call and get rejected, then you'll be highly unlikely to create positive future call results. Who wants to experience repeated rejection? In this example, you've already created a mental image of rejection. You've mentally *seen* the rejection and so those feelings of being rejected overwhelm you, even though you haven't made a single call.

Now, logically you know the call hasn't happened. And logically, you know that there may be a variety of outcomes. But lacking a mental image that leads to a positive outcome, you may be creating a mental strategy that leads to an undesirable outcome (or avoiding the calls all together). What if you were to envision yourself making the sale and create a personal mental strategy that leads to those good feelings, *then* make the call?

The key to staying motivated is keeping a positive mental image that leads to positive outcomes. If you imagine that you will achieve your desired outcome, those images will motivate you to do so. Consider Christmas. When you were a child, I imagine that it was like pulling teeth to get you out of bed 364 days a year. However, if you celebrated Christmas, on December 25th, you were likely the first person up, probably before daylight, anticipating that positive outcome.

Just Do It!

Nike uses a unique understanding of the human psyche. They know that people (literally) look up when they are creating mental images. It's likely one of the reasons that Nike frequently employs billboards and building murals. You look *up* at them. Nike recognizes that people are motivated by good feelings and they want people to take action and consistently create those positive feelings. (I ran a mile, hit a home run, scored the game-winning goal ...) "Just do it!"

Similarly, most of us sub-vocalize when we read. By this I mean that as you read a book, you hear character voices in your head. So when you read the words "just do it," Nike has nudged you by using the voice already in your head. Or, like the old freeway diner signs, "Eat at Joe's." Gee, I'm hungry. I guess I should eat at Joe's. In business, your call to action might be "sign up now." Does that mean everyone will sign up? Of course not. Not everyone buys or has bought Nike products either. But I like their odds.

The words in Nike advertising are simply the frosting on the cake. They foremost create *visual* and *mental* images of success. Instead of using a passel of adjectives like "comfortable, reliable, or durable," to hawk their wares, they show images of the *outcome* that Nike products help produce. Nike is expert at weaving this strategy into their marketing. At creating positive mental images. "Imagine you can," "you're doing great," "winners envision success." The feeling of positive motivation is associated with the Nike brand; "Just Do It" is simply the word representation.

And Then ...

Let's say you're driving to meet friends at a recommended restaurant. You are using GPS, making the restaurant easy to locate. While this is a simple concept–going from place A to place B–it's not used often enough in achieving personal or professional goals.

As discussed earlier, not knowing what you want is your first challenge. If you don't identify important goals and milestones, you can't create a map to get you there. A person might move, using educated guesses (or randomly), towards what they believe will lead to their perceived (yet unstated) goals. Maybe they get there, maybe they don't. Maybe they won't even know if they did or not. In other words–they stumble through life's opportunities blindfolded.

It's comparable to gazing at a mountain summit, thinking; "I'd like to be up there," so you start hiking. During your trek, you see the peak in the distance, but perhaps you run out of energy or lose your way. I guarantee though, if a helicopter dropped you off at the summit, you would do whatever it took to make it safely back down. And once you found your way down, you would know the path up. (There's a reason hindsight is 20/20.)

Okay. You've made it back down, mapped out the mountain, and are now able to successfully navigate it. Bingo. Reverse engineering at its most basic. It's the prime reason why inventors and companies seek to protect their intellectual property with patents. (Once a technology is introduced, there are aggressive, cunning companies waiting to take it apart and emulate it.) Know your goals. Use your mental GPS and create a step by step action plan to get there. Summing up:

- Create your action plan for success. You use a GPS to find a restaurant, so why would you expect to achieve desired personal or professional success without a similar path?

- Create the path. The most effective way is work from the goal backwards. How do you find a store in an unfamiliar mall? You stop at the directory to determine the path from where you are to where you want to be.

- Follow through. It's up to you to make it happen.

Spychology.

In military parlance, reconnaissance is a mission to obtain information. Making observations for strategic purposes. In this guide, we're talking life reconnaissance. You're going to be doing a lot of exploring, observing, investigating, and examining of your life. Where you want it to go, how you'll get there, and how you'll know when you find it. You're going to do a bit of spying on yourself, becoming a spychologist in your own life.

Being a spychologist means being *present* in your own life. To examine and determine—with microscopic precision—your own actions and who you are. Step into your life. *Spy on yourself.* Be in a relationship with yourself. Learn what makes you happy, sad, crabby, elated, depressed, content. Do that and the rest will take care of itself (but not *by* itself).

"If you question something generally accepted as fact, you must also question the source that denies that fact."

~ Michael

Showtime.

As a successful musician you've logged thousands of practice hours. You were great and imaginative sitting at the piano this morning, sounded fantastic in the green room an hour before the show, and have given hundreds of public performances. But tonight an eager audience will judge you anew. People who arranged babysitters and rearranged their social calendars. People who shared their evening plans with social media friends. People preparing to form their lasting opinion of you. Tonight, you begin at square one.

This is a reminder that throughout life people will be forming their impression of you. While your first impression is most lasting, don't overlook the lasting impression that you'll reinvent throughout life. It's a hurdle to overcome a poor initial impression and a struggle to continually live up to a wonderful first impression.

Some labels you'll earn, on some you'll feel short-changed, with many—it won't matter to you one way or the other. The best you can do is live life for you. On your journey, be cognizant of your personal fame so that those you touch form a warm and unforgettable impression. Make a resolute effort to always bring your "A" game. It'll bring joy to your life whether anyone else notices or not.

"Doing things for others just to get them to like you is prostituting yourself. You have to like yourself first. Why strip for your own money?"

I'll huff and I'll huff and I'll – "*Oh, no you won't!*"

Physically and spiritually you're about as strong and resilient as you work to be. However, unlike the story of the three little pigs, if not erected on a solid foundation and built using good technique, a real life brick structure can crumble, lean, and eventually topple. Huuum. A lot like life.

There aren't a lot of shortcuts in constructing a long-lasting brick house, but it's never too late to start (check out those Tower of Pisa repairs). The piggy lesson? Hard work, attention to yourself and your needs, and dedication to your goals pays off. While the first two pigs tossed their abodes together quickly to have more play time, the third pig carefully created a plan and followed through in the construction. The efforts paid off handsomely. By looking ahead and creating a long-term solution, piggy number three is better prepared to weather life's inevitable storms, the occasional bad guy, enjoy and a comfy fireplace to sit near (rather than in).

Now, here's a secret. All three pigs could have built using bricks and still faced similar results as they did with their straw and wood abodes. It could also be said that a straw or stick house could be built that would be as lasting as brick. It begins with the foundation, your attention to detail and craftsmanship, and continues on through your focus on the desired outcome. Huuum. Just like life.

"It is not the beauty of a building you should look at; it's the construction of the foundation that will stand the test of time."

~ David Allan Coe

Wake up, again.

Humans are fickle. We freeze in the winter and roast in the summer. We appreciate the summer in the winter and the winter in the summer. Many people living in cold climates complain long and hard about the harsh winters. But the first time the temperature broaches 60 degrees (Fahrenheit), all bets are off. It's as though the bracing cold, snow, and ice was never there, and not a thought is given to moving to a warmer climate. Out of coat, out of mind.

Though we live in days, weeks, and years, we remember in glimpses, flashes, and moments. Life unfolds before us like a movie, yet we remember it as photographs; recalling not the day of the week but a fraction of a second of the minute. We don't grasp the vastness of the ocean, yet remember the taste of the breath-stealing gulps of saltwater.

We learn to appreciate what we have by what we've lost. What we love by what fills our hearts and by having had our hearts broken in the past. How to overcome loss and accept love. How to value the people in our life by those that are gone. How to accept life's bitter hardships knowing that a new season awaits. We are fearful of those who want to take a part of us away, yet yearn to find that person or thing that will do just that. While living in the present, don't forget what brought you to this day. A giddy, childlike innocence is a wonderful thing to wake up to. Rain or shine, winter or summer.

"Make love of life the love of your life. With a little finagling, it all falls into place after that."

13

Forge your trail.

Like sheep, we stand in a never-ending lines without so much as a hint of what awaits once (if) we make our way to the front. Why? It's akin to sitting–idling–in traffic. You'd avoid it if you could, accelerate around it, walk, bike–you'd consider all known alternatives. So why the sheep mentality of doing things simply because it seems like what everyone else is doing?

In 1923, a *New York Times* reporter asked mountaineer George Mallory why he climbed Mt. Everest. Mallory responded, "Because it's there." Those three words have been an oft-appropriated quote for more than 90 years; used to describe everything from the moon landing to eating a 72 ounce steak. But it makes a poor excuse for standing in a line just because "everyone else is."

Leave the line. Find your own destination, forge your own trail, make your own memories. You'll succeed. You'll fail. You'll love. You'll live. What you won't do, is stare at the back of someone else's head, shuffling along an inch or two at a time, biding your time, waiting for death.

"My mind is in a state of constant rebellion. I believe that will always be so."
~ George Mallory

Hey you! Yes, you. I'm right here!

People sit a few feet from each other and use social media to communicate with each other. It's a parody we see played out over and again. Yet, here we are. Hordes are tethered to their devices (no, not you, of course not). It's part of society and will continue to evolve. Sometimes I wonder if our social skills are eroding in pace with technology. Face-to-face communication is becoming rarer by the day and any remaining people skills are being boiled down to contractions, abbreviations, emoticons, and 140 characters.

I ask you this: *When was the last time you sent a text or email just to say "I'm thinking of you" or "I love you?"* No requests for grocery store runs, buying gas, or picking up dry cleaning. Simply, "I love you." Now that is a powerful use of social media. And with 140 characters you can take a few seconds to add a sincere "I can't wait to see you!" I have a feeling there are already throngs of tweens and teens doing so. Time for the adults to step up.

"Just as dinosaurs didn't evolve and became extinct, the world as we know it isn't changing – it's disappearing."

~ Michael

There's only one *you.*

Creating a new flower variety is an admirable accomplishment. Unless you believe otherwise. Making a billion dollars in the stock market is staggering. Unless money doesn't matter to you. It's all relative and that's what makes us simultaneously both unique and clichéd.

We gravitate towards those with similar interests–stock clubs, horticultural societies, Kiwanis, scouting, bead collectors, hiking, biking, TV, movies, etc. But that doesn't mean a horticulturist can't enjoy tinkering with V-twin motorcycle engines. In fact, we are so good at stereotyping people that a hybrid-flower-growing horticulturist covered in tattoos and riding a motorcycle would seem odd to some. So what! As Marion Davies wrote in her 1975 autobiography, *The Times We Had*, "An imitator is always a poor example."

Is imitation the sincerest form of flattery? Imitation is certainly popular (see Las Vegas), but is poor example of originality. Many of us like to stay current on fashion and hair trends. Some of us want the fastest car. All of which imitates an original idea, thus leading to trends.

Some people outwardly eschew popular trends and consequently create more in their wake. We demonstrate individuality–tattoos, piercings, purple hair, etc.–until we look like all the other people with tattoos, piercings, and purple hair, once again finding ourselves in a long line of imitators. But there is individualism within sameness. Your tattoo may be completely different than any others. Your taste in art, while art, may be very obscure and (at least momentarily) unique. Maybe you are original simply by not doing anything and thus are the one person in your cliché (there we go again) that doesn't imitate or follow what everyone else is doing.

You don't like a band? Find another. Or better yet, create your own music. An artist selling 20,000,000 copies of their latest work doesn't mean you have to be the 20,000,001st to buy it.

We go to school. We learn. We read. We experiment. We have Aha! moments. Those "now I get it!" forehead slapping epiphanies. We get diplomas, degrees, awards, and recognition. After all that experience comes your opportunity to write the next textbook. Your thoughts. Your ideas. Your art. Your music. You didn't invent the words or the musical notes–you arrange them in your own unique way. Reading "the black cat" then writing "the black cat" is merely an imitation. A copy of what has been done. Where's the "palm-sized kitten, once white as a snowball, now black as a Halloween cat as it was carried from the burning house?"

Next up, the king (and his aping court)! Let's get right to it. Elvis is dead. Period. And Elvis impersonators should recognize that admirers are actually seeking a connection to another human, long since passed. But: No Elvis = no imitators. Thus an industry was born.

It takes similar effort and energy to develop an individual style and voice as it does trying to pretend to be someone else. Learn to be yourself and save the aping for weekend parties. Be Elvis; not the guy on the sidewalk *pretending* to be Elvis. And where are you on the trend ladder? A setter or an imitator? What is inside you yearning to be set free? Surely to be more than a replica of someone else. Then why the sheep mentality? Perhaps it's because there's often more confidence–more faith–in imitating those who have already blazed original trails. Imitating the accepted and desired rather than risk rejection or ridicule of the original self. The problem is–imitators are always poor examples.

We watch actors because ... wait for it ... they are pretending to be other people. Same with spin-offs and sequels. To many, *Star Trek: The Next Generation*, is superior to the original series. But it exists only *because* of the original.

"Live the life that has people wanting to be you. Not the other way around."

~ Michael

If the faucet drips, turn it on.

Boredom serves a purpose. If nothing, it's an opportune time to challenge yourself.

Is your body or soul trying to teach or guide you toward something? To get off your rear and make new discoveries? To use the time as personal reflection? Often, it's simple laziness that paves the path to boredom. You laze around, doing nothing, then become frustrated because you're bored. Boredom can become a forced idleness—a *belief* that you've nothing to do with your time (and of course, your time is also your life). Let's get this straight: quiet times and solitude are not analogous with boredom. Boredom is a pause. A time to consider what you want to do with your time.

Being idle or "bored" from time to time is perfectly natural. Thinking times. Quiet times. But one of the red flags with long or frequent periods of boredom is that disillusionment, self-pity, and depression are usually right on its heels. One of the easiest remedies for non-clinical boredom is curiosity. And if you look at it that way, boredom is a choice. A choice sometimes made out of fear. There are likely many things you want to do, try, and experience but haven't because you are afraid you'll fail. The price of that fear includes boredom which, if not addressed, draws you towards that icy path of disillusionment and self-pity.

What do you do when you are bored? What would you do if you weren't afraid? What would you suggest to others? And why aren't you doing it? If you wait till you are one hundred percent confident that everything is a bazillion percent just the way you want and believe it should be before doing anything, you might as well grab a beverage and lawn chair and watch from the sideline while everyone else enjoys the game of life. It's like saying you don't want to learn how to walk until you know where you are going. It doesn't work that way. You have to be ready for opportunity when it comes. In fact, you have to make your own opportunities.

You don't have to learn you're dying to begin living. Seems obvious, but it's what many of us do. The uncomfortable fact is that it's really, really easy to wait until we learn we're dying before we start living. Guess what. We are all physically dying. A little bit every day. You may only be as old as you feel, but the calendar begs to differ. Don't put off your should-haves would-haves, because you don't know when you're going run out of opportunities. In lay terms—get off your ass and do something. The water won't flow until you turn the faucet on.

"Boredom: the desire for desires."

~ Leo Tolstoy

If your wallet contains only money, you're broke.

Multi-billionaire Warren Buffett once shared his sentiment about "stuff" during an interview with talk show host and journalist Charlie Rose. "I have every possession I want. I have a lot of friends who have a lot more possessions. But in some cases, I feel the possessions possess them, rather than the other way around."

While Buffett may live in the same house as he did in 1958, he's still a multi-billionaire and one of the world's richest people. While he's to be applauded for pledging to give away the vast majority of his wealth, most of this charity will happen after his death. You know–when he no longer wants or needs it (tongue planted firmly in cheek).

Things look different from twelve inches than from twelve feet or twelve miles. Obvious, but we tend to judge, and make decisions, from our most convenient perspective. Then you skydive for the first time. The odds of loading your pants exponentially lessen the closer you get to the safety of terra firma. At 3,000 feet, you adamantly and loudly pray to your God that you'll never, ever, ever sin again. After a safe landing, all prayers are presumed answered and promptly forgotten. "Need" again becomes "want."

It's a hell of a lot easier to possess a benevolent attitude when you have little or nothing, and an incredibly difficult habit to maintain once your coffers are full. When what was once luxury becomes necessity. When thankfulness takes a backseat to greed.

Time for some perspective. What do HD, 3D, and flat screen TVs, your smart phone, and laptop or tablet have in common? They are all things many consider necessities, yet none were available just twenty-five years ago. Facebook? Began in 2004. Twitter? 2006. Pinterest and Instagram? Seemingly eons ago, back in 2010. So, are these wants or needs? If you want to conduct a poll, you'll need to do so via snail mail (spotty) or in person with the more than 40% of the world population that does not have internet access.

It's hard to miss something you've never had. You can long for something. Yearn for it even if you've never had it, but you can't rightly miss it. Once it's in your grasp or possession though–whole new ballgame. Jay Leno didn't know he needed a Rolls-Royce till he owned a Ford Pinto, and now, the rarer the vehicle, the more he lusts for it. And that's okay. A healthy respect or admiration for possessions (for lack of a better term) is great. And really, no one can tell you where to spend your discretionary time or financial resources. Like Warren Buffett said, just remember who possesses whom.

I want that Rolls-Royce. I have to have that house. I can't wait until I have ... and so it goes, until we have it all. The carrot in front of the stick masterfully performing its duty. And there's *always* a carrot. Those things that were once a luxury are now simply a part of everyday life. The 5 bedroom house now needs a 6th. The car that accelerates from 0–60 mph in 5.8 seconds now needs to do so in 3.9.

The rewards and fruit of our labor are meant to be enjoyed. But if the toys are the primary reason to play the game, then it really is just a game. Happiness doesn't come in a wallet. It might bring fleeting satisfaction. But, give pause. When you lay your head down to sleep, does it matter whether there is a Ford or a

Ferrari in your garage or even that you have a garage? Maybe so. No harm in that. But be able to explain to yourself why. Not to others, to yourself.

"As a man rises in the world, his luxuries of yesterday become today's necessities."

~ E.R. Jackman and R.A. Long, *The Oregon Desert*

Roasted crickets, anyone?

How can you say you're missing something if you've never experienced it? Food is a terrific example. "I don't like chocolate covered scarab beetles." How about roasted crickets? No? Is it because it seems disgusting or because you've actually tried them? In many parts of the world, bugs and insects are part of an everyday diet. In Thailand, as example, it's common to prepare and eat grasshoppers, crickets, and woodworms.

What would it take for you to be open and change your mindset to something like, "I can't wait to try this!" or, "I wonder what that tastes like?" Where is your key that would help you make that thought transformation? Who holds it? The obvious answer to who, is *you*. Less obvious is who is using it and why. Frequently, the answer isn't a person but an emotion or internal conflict. Usually self-doubt or fear.

Fear, anxiety, self-doubt. Strong emotions, but they do not characterize who you are as a person. To allow (in this instance, negative) emotions to control your actions, is to willingly hand that negativity your key. Recognize the feelings, but also know that they will pass, can be conquered (or at least corralled) and your being—your life—will continue under your command.

Of course, none of us will entirely tame all of our fears. Those quirky ones, those based on experience, and those living solely in our imagination. Experience is a great teacher. We learn not to touch a hot stove or play with matches. We can then choose to be afraid of flames and hot stoves or use them to our advantage. It's the fears living in our imagination that are toughest to wrangle.

Fear is an emotional excuse that can keep you from pursuing your goals. Facing fear starts with recognizing that your desires, dreams, and goals are more important and significant in your life than any obstacle. While avoidance is an easy option, remember that what you are too afraid to attempt will weigh you down more than any failed venture you tackle. Failing at least demonstrates a willingness. It's a badge that you participate in life. It also means there is one less obstacle on your way to achieving your desires and goals. Maybe you'll succeed next time out. Maybe not. Guess what. For the most part, nobody except you cares one way or the other. It's a big world and everyone is concerned with their own life. As you should be with yours. It's a busy world filled with billions of busy people. No one is focused on you like you. That provides you all the autonomy you might want, as well as all the attention you might someday seek. Self-permission is a wonderful thing.

If someone tells you that they are completely focused on your happiness, and you buy in, you'll find yourself taking advice from a broken person who has yet to find their own place in life. Take a step back. Should you really expect someone to live for no reason other than to please you? I'm sure on the surface that that sounds fantastic, but how can someone make you happy if they can't be happy without you? That's not a partner. That's a stalker.

"If you allow fear and self-doubt to hold the key to your life, your biggest failure will be never knowing whether you would have succeeded."

Listen Up!

If you say "I'm listening," say it with a straight face and because you mean it. Saying "I'm listening" while you're really watching TV or playing a video game, and responding with "yes honey," will come back and bite you on the bottom. If you say you're listening.... *listen.*

Okay, the TV is off. Now, are you listening to what is being said or to what you want to hear? Throughout life, you'll need to be willing to hear, and listen to, a number of incredibly disagreeable opinions. Why? Because if you say, "that's the stupidest thing I've ever heard" or "you're wrong," you'll never get anything out of that person again. You don't have to agree with someone to appreciate that what they have to say is important to them. Moreover, you'll never hear what *isn't* being said, if you aren't actively listening.

Here's a brief Personal Listening 101 course presented in fewer than thirty words*: One of the most sincere acts of respect is listening to what someone has to say. You'll learn a lot more by listening than by talking.*

"Most people do not listen with the intent to understand; they listen with the intent to reply."

~ Stephen R. Covey

Challenge your assumptions.

If you're looking for it–you'll find it. If you don't believe it exists, it can easily be hidden from you. It's a natural tendency to see what we want to see, find what we want to find, and validate it over and again as fact. Magicians bank on it. It's why hiding in plain sight works. But there are glaring exceptions. Let's face it–a burly longshoreman keeping a bookshelf filled with "creative dress patterns" is going to draw attention. Why? Didn't meet our internal stereotype. But as long as we can rationally justify something, we are mentally willing to accept it as a given.

People suffering from Schizophrenia or other mental disorders often see things that the rest of us believe aren't there. This is referred to as having a *visual hallucination*–a false sensory experience. It can also be an auditory experience—hearing things we don't.

Specialists diagnose and confirm the phenomenon with regularity. But what if it's the rest of us that simply aren't seeing things that perhaps *are* there? Not drawing any medical conclusions, just suggesting that it's worthwhile to challenge the assumption. Just because we don't see something doesn't mean it isn't there.

What if these hallucinogenic episodes are transition phases where a person nearing death experiences something open and available only to them? Possibly life's way of easing us into the next chapter; whatever that may be. Implausible? Maybe. But discounting it as impossible is just an answer of convenience. For instance, we have a tendency to accept people at face value who say that they've had a near death experience (e.g., seeing a bright white light or floating over their body during surgery). Yet because dementia patients often can't sufficiently articulate for themselves, we tend to question their rationality.

Does validation require physical evidence or simply a belief? Families of dementia patients may opt to pray for their loved ones (to an entity some people believe does not exist). Without proof, why not pray to Casper? (Because *that* would be foolish?) Many accept their personal religion because it "simply *must* be," while questioning the religious beliefs of others as being "simply *impossible*." Countless wars are fought in the name of religion; alas, another topic altogether.

Life makes it alarmingly easy to believe what we want to believe. Other people seeing objects or people that do not mesh with an "ordinary" belief system can be frightening and is usually, and conveniently, labeled a disease symptom. It remains a mystery and a door easily left closed, rather than consider the possibility that *we* are the blind ones. We filter out what we do not (or choose not) to believe. Perhaps our own filters fade as we transition towards passing (and I'm in no hurry to find out!).

So yes, it is possible, perhaps even probable, that those suffering dementia are reacting to someone or something that isn't there. But, what if? *Challenge your assumptions*. Because ... what if?

"*The eyes see only what the mind is prepared to comprehend.*"
~ French philosopher, Henri Bergson

Life is your autobiography.

In school and professional life, there are books you read because you have to. Some are boring, some loosely interesting, most providing you with necessary knowledge. In life, there are books you read because you can't put them down. You can't wait to turn the page to see what happens next.

Both type of books add value to life. Some lasting, some lessons, some memories, some on your bookshelf and in your mind for a lifetime. If you were a book, what would it be? In what section or genre of the library would you be found? What stories would it contain? What lessons would you be teaching? What sights, smells, emotions, and voices do you want your readers to experience? What learning moments do you want to share? What do you want people to remember? What legacy are you writing today? You'll be surprised at the book inside of you.

"A teacher affects eternity; he can never tell where his influence stops."

~ Henry Adams

If you make the Kool-Aid, drink the Kool-Aid.

Okay, so you're writing your life book. What words of wisdom will you offer? Consider: If you could mentor any person—living or dead, famous, infamous, or other (excluding family or partner)—who would it be? Why? What would you want to instill? What advice would you offer? What difference would you hope to make? What would you want to change or affect? What would you want them to learn?

Answering those questions shines a light on what's important to you as well as what qualities you believe you should strengthen. George Bernard Shaw wrote, "He who can, does. He who cannot, teaches." Here though, it's more of, "He who doesn't, preaches." All the things you believe you should do in life are the first words of wisdom you'll proffer to others. But offering advice that you refuse to take yourself is like the Pope giving instructions on the Karma Sutra. It doesn't really hold much credence. Sit down, make a list of all those things you want to tell others to do, then go do them.

"Everyone you will ever meet knows something you don't."

~ Bill Nye

Setting the table.

If the Jeopardy answer is "What *can* you bring to it + what *will* you bring to it + *why* will you bring it," the question is, 'What is the table?'"

It's a common question. "What do you bring to the table?" Many have been asked during a job interview and certainly many of us have wondered it about others. We seek to fill voids. To complement ourselves. You shouldn't change who you are to be with another person but do take time for a personal relationship inventory. Perhaps what you *can* bring to the table–education, stable home, credit score, etc.–is fantastic and you are rightfully proud of your achievements and accomplishments. So what. It falls on deaf ears if it's not what a potential partner is seeking, if they place no importance on it, or already possess it. No void was filled. No complementary angle discovered.

What you can bring to the table isn't necessarily synonymous with what you *will* bring to the table. Certainly, you'll want to sift through your attributes and selectively present your best and most desirable characteristics, without deceit. You might choose to omit things you've been working to diminish or end. Smoking is an easy example. You can choose to bring a pack of cigarettes to the table but you don't have to.

Like any good salesperson, you need to know the other person's hot buttons and consider what they are looking to find in their (life or professional) partner. You must then perform a personal inventory to determine if you can (or want to) fulfill those needs. Relationships are built on mutual satisfaction, respect, and commitment. Example–let's say you have a classic 1965 Rolls-

Royce Silver Shadow for sale. You found someone that absolutely loves it. Fulfills their transportation needs, their Jay Leno-esque desire for autos, everything they could hope for. But, they don't have the cash. They are not at a place in their life where they are able to complete the transaction. No deal. In the long run, that's a good thing. Entering into a transaction (relationship) where one party is unwilling or unable to contribute is a lose/lose. Even though you could still hand over the keys to the Rolls, you won't.

There's always a difference between what you inherently bring to the table and what another person is looking for. Nothing and no one will ever meet one hundred percent of your requirements nor those of your potential partner (they're called fairy tales for a reason). We began with what you can bring to the table, separated the wheat from the chaff, and determined what those qualities are and what you will want to bring. Now we are now ready to tackle the next part of the equation. "Why?" What are you looking to achieve? A lifelong loving relationship? A great friendship? Understanding *why* you load your backpack with chosen items enables you to most effectively reach for and achieve your goals.

One last, crucial thing: be honest in your assessment. And of yourself. Don't go into any relationship with the hope or anticipation of changing another person. That's just lighting the resentment fuse on a time bomb that will burn over time and eventually, inevitably explode. To summarize:

- What can you bring to the table?
- What will you bring to the table?
- Why? What is your goal?

All foundations eventually settle.

You've probably heard people say something along the lines of, "She's just settling for him. She could do so much better." Are you afraid that you might "settle?" That you will miss that proverbial soulmate? Would they have been the next person you met? Do you play the "what if" game? "What if I'd waited for the next person?" "What if I've settled for someone lesser than who I might have been with (hello, ego calling)?" "What if I'm not *in* love with the person?" On the other hand, if we don't "take who we can get" we worry that someone would leave our life that possibly was meant to be our partner, but failed to either set off the initial fireworks, or the fireworks came to a sputtering stop.

What are the signs? Unfortunately not usually as obvious as a resounding "this sucks!" It creeps up on you. One minute the floors are level, the next, you're living in a weird building in Pisa. In your love relationship, settling is that little difference between someone that makes you smile and that special someone that brings you smiles. A cute joke can bring a smile once. Maybe a few times. But it takes a lot of material to stand on someone's stage for a lifetime.

Maybe it isn't really "settling" that is the challenge. Maybe it's complacency. Take the opportunity to continually reinvent your relationship. Work on creating and developing your material together and perform it in its continuing evolution through time for your world stage. Always fresh and vibrant. And don't mistake contentment for settling. Contentment can include that single smile because you know so many more will be coming.

On Being Congruent.

S.O.L. = Spiritually out of line. (Not what you were thinking?) Being spiritually out of line is when your heart and your soul–your essence–are not congruent with your actions.

Most of us can tell when someone isn't being congruent. That is to say, most of us can tell the difference between sincerity and someone just going through the motions or trying to B.S. us. Their actions don't match their words or perhaps they are sincere in their words but then don't follow up with action that is agreeable with those words.

Being congruent and walking the walk isn't always easy. Taking the necessary (often difficult) steps to inspire positive outcomes can be emotionally consuming, and, of course, there is more than simple words involved.

In personal relationships as example, you might tell that special person you love them and that they are everything that you've ever, ever wanted in a mate. Everyone wants to be loved so there is a tendency to want to believe we are loved when we hear it. But after all is said, it'll be your actions that do the talking. Anyone needing proof of this need only to spend a little time in a small cage with a hungry, agitated lion. You won't know what he's saying, but I guarantee you'll understand his actions and intent.

Much of this is brought about by the desire for immediate or short-term gratification. People say things they don't mean or intend to follow through on once they "make the sale." This is obviously detrimental to the long term success of a relationship (business or personal) unless the intent is to truly be a one-off, fly-by-night kind of thing. And even if that is the case, have the hard talk up front. Explain yourself and your intentions (lots of people rolling their eyes about now, I suspect). If not, it only hurts others and you will eventually be bitten by your own beast. (Karma's a bitch, as the saying goes.) Don't shortchange yourself or anyone else. Everyone out there deserves at least that much.

"It is well to remember that the entire population of the universe, with one trifling exception, is composed of others."

~Andrew J. Holmes

It ain't all pixie dust and unicorns, my friends.

How would you measure your dreams if they became real? Those special dreams where the knight slays the frightening dragon and saves the damsel. When the drop dead gorgeous woman or handsome man walks into your life. Dreams and reality don't always co-exist as we … well … *dream* that they will.

Sometimes life just doesn't want to play along. Does that mean you failed? Not really. You can give and give and give to someone and still get burned. Some people are users, don't really care, or still haven't found (or even know) what it is they are looking for. It is not your job to fix them. It *is* your "job" to be kind and loving. If another doesn't reciprocate, then so be it. Don't beat yourself up for being a loving, kind person.

And remember: you can't measure a dream by the moment you believe it becomes real. It can only be measured when it becomes real for both you *and* your dreamboat. Certainly not in the yearning phase when everything is roses, rainbows, and pixie dust. That's still part of an ongoing dream—not reality. Lust to love doesn't happen overnight, sometimes it doesn't happen at all, and probably not in the way you dreamed it would. Time is the great awakener. The final ingredient.

"Don't let anyone steal your dream. It's your dream, not theirs."

~ Dan Zadra

Get your own damn coffee.

Interns get a bad rap. For the opportunity to gain experience they deliver mail, grab coffee, and make-believe their mentor has achieved God status. Thing is, we are all interns in our own lives. Most of us get our own coffee. We shill for things. The difference is that by being your own intern, you gain the *all* the benefits.

When it comes to your personal life, how about bypassing the middleman and going straight to *you*? Listen to what others have to offer, observe life around you, and absorb what you can. The lessons are ripe for the picking. Just don't give up *you* for *them*. You don't have to be the person who gets coffee for a prima donna simply because she is going through caffeine withdrawal. Users depend on people that don't have the will to be themselves. Being an intern means being open to knowledge and discovery. Not being subservient. Be an intern in your own life.

"Live life as an observer but not a spectator. Learn the rules, get in the game, break some rules. Live. Experience. There is no exhilaration to be achieved sitting on the bench."

~ Michael

You know what they say about opinions.

It takes courage to be honest and tact to be liked after you've exercised the courage. Employing a bit of tact doesn't change facts, but it goes a long way towards massaging things in your favor. How? Simple: No one likes an ass. At the same time, people seldom respect an ass-kisser. Enter, tact. Honesty, openness, respect, and a belief in your opinion *and* consideration for others. Diplomacy should always precede any fear of war.

Here's an example: A friend is excited about a book they have read and loans it to you. When you return it you might be tempted to (honestly) say, "That book was a complete, boring snoozer that I thought would never end," or, you could simply reply, "It wasn't my style, but it is well written."

Sometimes though, regardless of how you approach things *it's* going to happen. You will rub someone wrong way. You may not even know the person well. Maybe you called a kid ugly before realizing it is their child. Maybe you cut them off in traffic and then found yourself on the same elevator. Or didn't hold the elevator door. These days it doesn't take much.

So yes, you will be considered an ass at various times throughout life. Just try and earn the moniker; for your own reasons and for reasonable principles. Sometimes others grow or come around to seeing your view. Don't count on it and don't depend on it. Being an ass isn't all it's cracked up to be. It's hard sticking to your principles and, often, a person's base reaction is simply, "Ignore him, he's just an ass." You can't please everyone. But pleasing yourself at someone else's expense? Well, that is just being an ass and you'll suffer the consequences. You have to be able to look yourself in the mirror. Being an ass is not subject to age. I've met just as many 76 year old overly honest individuals as I have 16 year olds. People can have an *assitude* at any age.

You know, it's okay to just be you. It's the people who try to make you be who *they* are (or want you to be), that create sandstorms. Just be yourself and surround yourself with people that celebrate the individual in each of us. Be kind. Please yourself and be kind to the mirror as well. We're all in this together. There is no "them." Only "us." While you're living in life's campground—pick up after yourself. Help your neighbors. Don't be a distraction. Don't play with matches. Don't leave an unattended fire. Don't. Be. An. Ass.

No matter what you do though, no matter how hard you try to be agreeable, you are going to piss off someone, somewhere. They'll eventually forget, but you have to live with you forever. Remember too, others are struggling with demons of their own. Maybe they arc just having a bad day. Then again, maybe they're just an ass. It'll be left for you to decide, just as others will form their opinion of you.

"*Sometimes being a nice person is all about knowing when to be an asshole.*"

~ John Cheese

Pick any two.

Your bosses' boss strolls through the workplace and everyone is either hush-hush or kissing his heinie. It's as if the messiah himself has chosen to specifically walk among you. But, if you didn't know the person and they cut you off in traffic, you'd be apt to scream every obscenity in the book while steering with your knees, flipping them the bird with one hand, and laying so hard on the horn with your other that your palm would have the car logo permanently imprinted on it.

Context. Oh, that, and the whole money thing. Here's a secret. You, your boss, and your bosses' boss are all made out of the same thing. Just different people with different jobs. You showed they were no different when your middle finger jutted up like a space shuttle at launch when you didn't know them and they had no control over your wallet. Yup ... the three things that most of our compasses spin to at one time or another. Power. Control. Money.

Where does your mental compass point? What is your magic lure? Is it money? Power? A contented life? Unlike earth's magnetic compass, you can point yours in whichever direction(s) you choose. Remember though, it can be difficult to juggle eight balls at a time. As the saying goes: "Fast, good, cheap. Pick any two." Choose carefully.

"Some people are born to life heavy weights, some are born to juggle golden balls."

~ Max Beerbohm

Human Branding.

Why would a person pay $7,600 USD for a Gucci brand shoulder bag, but not consider the same bag for 25 bucks if it was offered at Wal-Mart? No differences in workmanship, materials, or quality. Literally the exact same bag–different store, different label. Why? Perceived value.

We're accustomed to Gucci demanding big bucks and Wal-Mart being "affordable." Gucci set the expectation that their products are worth thousands of dollars just as Wal-Mart has set the expectation of "Always Low Prices." At the time of this writing, the number one search result for "low prices" is, you guessed it, Wal-Mart. Top of the search list for "designer shoulder bags" ... Gucci.

Gucci doesn't sell as many bags as Wal-Mart, but then again, Gucci doesn't have to or want to. They sell to their demographic. Their audience. They have carefully crafted their image as an upscale, expensive, desirable brand and people respond accordingly.

What's your brand? What are you projecting to the world? People will take you at your own sense of self-worth and your own perceived value. Whatever your personal brand, make it yours. Own it.

" We are leashed by societal norms, defined by our willingness to conform, but limited only by our imagination."

~ Michael

Who are you anyway?

Isn't it a miserable thing when others refuse to acknowledge your brilliance? When they can't see your unassailable reasoning and logic? Life sure is easier when it's unanimously agreed that you are the cock of the walk. The center of the galaxy. Nay. The universe! The grand potentate.

Here's something to mull over: The moment you think you know everything–the moment you think you're all that–strap on some ass pads, because the gravel is going to burn on the way down. A healthy sense of self-worth and self-belief is essential. It's when it crosses from, "I am a good, loving, lovable, person with great attributes," to, "I know what is best for everyone, I'm right and everyone knows I'm right," that the problems creep in.

No matter how "all that" you might believe you are—even if your name is on the lips of every man, woman, and child in the United States of America—more than 96% of the planet would still have no clue who you are nor could they care less. Consider Shah Rukh Khan. He's an Indian actor, producer, and humanitarian with a net worth of more than $600 million (2nd most of any actor worldwide). Having made over eighty films, he's the most popular actor in India, a country with a population of more than 1.2 billion; nearly four times that of the United States. Never heard of him? Don't worry. He's never heard of you either. Funny how that works.

~ How much time have you wasted trying to change how people perceive you? ~

Less faking, more living.

There's a school of thought stating you should "fake it till you make it." A key problem with that is some people choose to fake it for a really, really, *really* long time, until faking it becomes a way of life: "Someday, I will ... till then, I'll pretend." At some point, you need to do something, to stop playing house, to stop lying to yourself and live the life you've been pretending to live. Believe me–living it is much more exhilarating than observing it. I guarantee the person giving their Academy Award acceptance speech is enjoying the moment much more than the person sitting in front of a TV staring at it. HD and surround sound won't help much either. You're still just one of millions of onlookers.

We've all fallen into this trap. Beguiled into believing that if we just *pretend* then all things magical and wonderful will happen. Orson Scott Card wrote about it in *Ender's Game*, "Perhaps it's impossible to wear an identity without becoming what you pretend to be." While I agree with the concept, my truth is that without action we are simply playing a game of make-believe.

Maybe you'll fool some of the people for an extended time. But you'll never fool yourself. And at the end of the day, if you are not true to yourself, then who are you? You can be a queen living in a moat-encircled, heavily fortified medieval castle guarded by throngs of Chris Hemsworth look-a-likes and I'll be Elvis singing to hordes of screaming fans. Nice role play and the makings of a great fiction essay. But, sorry, it's still make-believe. What will you do when Halloween is over?

It can take as much energy to create and live in a make-believe world as it does to create a life reality. You'll be surprised what you find burrowing and rooting around in the dark regions. Start with self-recognition. That you are more important than anyone else you might *pretend* to be. Use some imagination. Put your creativity into play. Like pretending? Study acting. Enjoy the sensation of soaring through the sky? Learn to fly. But pretending something doesn't make it so. You scrapped a knee once or twice, but aren't you glad you learned to ride a bike? You may have swallowed a pint or two of salt in your time, but you still love the beach, right? Dream your dreams, but live in your life.

"You can't wake a person who is pretending to be asleep."

~ Navajo proverb

It's all you, baby.

The mirror doesn't lie. Your hopes, your dreams, your desires ... your *you*. All staring right back at you. It's there, whether you see it (or want to) or not.

Are you waiting for something or someone to make our life whole? Guess what. That thing, that person is you. Look in the mirror. The person you see is the only person you will *always* have to navigate you through both calm and dangerous, turbulent waters.

Time to raise anchor, set sail, and experience your journey. What are you waiting for? Who is supposed to give you permission? (Hint: the answer is in the first paragraph.) It's your life. Period. You're at the helm and you control the rudder. Acknowledging and accepting this will deepen your relationships with others and strengthen your internal trust at the same time. Never be afraid to love, to risk failure, to grasp the successes as they come, to seek, learn, and to completely devour this life. Most important, along the way, never ever be afraid to trust in yourself.

No one could ever know you better than you already know yourself. Even so, life is an ongoing love affair with discovery and growth. It comes with it a multitude of teachers—most who mean well but may want to tell you what to do, how to do it, and when. You must remember that at the end of the day—you make the call. You pull the strings. As the saying goes, if you don't take control of your life, something or someone else will. Author Quentin Crisp said it best, "The consuming desire of most human beings is deliberately to plant their whole life in the hands of some other person." To this I will add three small (but immense) words: Don't. Do. That.

"The best way to find out if you can trust somebody is to trust them."

~ Ernest Hemingway

Hey, Mr. Know it all.

Do you need total conversational agreement from others before you can feel fully accepted for your beliefs? Is it enough for others to understand you or do you feel compelled to battle until you win agreement (knowing full well that many people will agree just to get you to shut-up, thus solving nothing)?

While we all enjoy sharing life's commonalities, it's a mistake to live wearing blinders. When two people agree on absolutely everything, one of them is unnecessary (or lying). Besides, blind acquiescence destroys opportunities for one to broaden their perspectives and to be who they really are. In the process, denying themselves experiences that foster a fuller, richer life.

For example, let's say I'm a classical music fanatic and have no appreciation for ragtime. The thing is, I don't need to enjoy it to appreciate the talent, thinking, and effort that went into its composition. Similarly, I may not "get" how Jackson Pollock, an influential American painter known for his unique style of drip painting, was considered a major figure in abstract expressionist art. But taking time to step into his shoes, his thinking, and his process will help me more fully appreciate the type of art that I do enjoy.

Accept knowing that you don't know everything and never will. Accept that you will not always be right, nor always wrong. Find solace in the quiet corners while appreciating others. You will learn things.

One of the things you will learn is the lesson of all that you don't know and have yet to discover and experience. If you think you know everything, or that you're always right, you'll quickly find solitude to be your only option. A verse in Buddhism's Dhammapada states, *"If while on your way you meet no one your equal or better, steadily continue on your way alone. There is no fellowship with fools."* And while there may be no fellowship with fools, a life of arrogance will soon corner you into a life with few alternatives.

I was recently chatting with a casual acquaintance who ended a depressing story of missed opportunity and inaction by saying, "I wish I'd known then what I know now." I replied, "Well, you know it now, and you just said it out loud for the whole world to hear. That excuse is gone. Now what?"

The conversation began when another friend (in her late-30's) said that she wished she'd had gone to college after finishing high school, adding that now she'd be in her 40's before graduating. I asked how old she'd be in four years if she chose not to fulfill her college dream. Another "reason" shattered.

In these cases, the argument was made that age (college) and life knowledge were *handicaps* to having and pursuing dreams and goals. The fact is, the opposite is true. Age and knowledge are tremendous assets and only become liabilities when used as excuses. As you get older, tell yourself, *"There's as much of life behind me as remains in front of me, but I'm determined to do more with what I have left, than what is left behind."*

The bottom line: You know now what you know now. But not as much as tomorrow. If you wait till you think you know everything, you'll never do anything. Pursue and devour knowledge. Even things that might seem trivial or meaningless when you come across them. You can't know if, or when, you'll need the information. Recognizing the word similarities between persecution and prosecution; scallops, scallions, and shallots; brothel and hostel; self-defecating and self-deprecating; or physalis (a flowering plant in the nightshade family) and syphilis are obvious. The knowledge of recognizing the *differences*: priceless.

"It is always too early to decide that it's too late."

~ Unknown

Wait just a minute, take just a minute.

I recently placed an online ad to give away a small table that was no longer being used (except to take up garage space). A gentleman responded to the ad, saying he could use the piece, was very was familiar with the area, and could come over right away.

Sure enough, about fifteen minutes later a muddy pick-up truck appeared and an old-timer backed it into the driveway. (Technically, he backed over some of the rockery and heather plants, but did eventually find the driveway.) After the table was loaded up, we made small talk for a few minutes. He asked how long I'd had the house and how I liked the neighborhood. Making a sweeping gesture towards the legion of firs and pine, he said he knew the area intimately because "I did all the trees around here." I was tempted to ask what he meant, but it was late and I was tired. I shook his hand and he went on his way.

I came inside, feeling terrible about dismissing him when I knew he'd have enjoyed the conversation and bending a friendly ear. But, I had mentally pulled the plug and went back into the house; content to watch his beater ramble down the street. Shame on me.

"I remind myself every morning: Nothing I say this day will teach me anything. So if I'm going to learn, I must do it by listening."

~ Larry King

Play Fair.

As kids, this was drummed into our heads. Our parents or guardians wanted us to be good sports, to follow the rules, to respect the feelings of others, to be gracious winners, and to handle losses with a congratulatory handshake to the winner.

What does it mean to play fair in adult life? Same. Don't hide stuff. Be honest. Don't blame others. If you mess up, admit it. Be happy for others. Stand up for yourself. Share. Be willing to eat crow every now and again. Remember there is homework due and things to learn and that others will grade you on it. Apologize. (Like getting a vaccination—the anticipation is worse than the action.)

And on those occasions you do apologize—be sincere (remember: no "buts"). So, what exactly is the difference between a sincere and insincere apology? Simply put, an insincere apology is nothing more than lip service. If somebody apologies and says "I shouldn't have said that," it may really mean "I shouldn't have said that *aloud.*" Another example would be, "I'm sorry you took it that way." This could be taken to mean, "Are you dense? You didn't understand a thing I said!"

How do you differentiate between sincere and insincere? Congruency. Recognize the power that words carry. You must believe in (and mean) your words. In the long run, even a hurtful message, if congruent and honestly communicated, is better than a lie. There is no progress where there is no honest meeting of the minds.

It's okay to speak your piece. Just remember, diplomacy goes a long way. Yes, you may hurt the other person, and yes, the consequences may be difficult to navigate. Do it upfront. Don't drag it out. Tell the truth faster. Then, take the time and work together to move forward. Like actor Robert Duvall said, "You just can't take a crash course to be a tango dancer in a movie."

"The reverse side also has a reverse side."

Fill 'er up?

The next time you are running around town, take notice of how many gas stations are located across from one other. On interstate roadways, it's a different story. There might only be one every hundred miles or so. Supply and demand dictates that those highway scarcities can charge more than their urban counterparts. But, when there are options, price is often a decisive factor. But not always. Sometimes they differentiate in other ways.

When was the last time you visited a gas station and an attendant cleaned your windshield? Never? Some of us are old enough to remember when a full-service attendant (really, they did exist!) would check your oil, tire pressure, and clean your windows. All while filling your tank.

Well, times change. Airlines charge you for legroom and checking bags. Some businesses try and charge you taxes on a tax you just paid. Service deteriorates and we start making noise about the lack of amenities and the way we are being treated. Sound familiar?

If you are operating a gas station, understand that there's a lot of competition. It's up to you to be the best gas station there is. Your customer (significant other) will notice and appreciate you for going the extra mile.

"I can't wear that (sheer negligee), people would think we aren't married!"

~ Wife to husband, *Rich & Strange* (1932, Alfred Hitchcock)

Faster, Faster, Faster··· SLOWER!

I was recently driving around running errands and a speed limit sign piqued my imagination. When we're driving, we follow rules of the road for our own safety as well as for those around us. In the case of speed limit signs, to gently nudge us to *slow down.*

Life goes by fast enough on its own. All the more reason not to speed through it. Listen to your internal clock. Develop and be mindful of your own speed limit signs. Enjoy the sunshine, rain, special moments, life's quirks and bumps. The stop sign will be there soon enough and unfortunately it doesn't come with a roundabout or U-Turn option. There's something to be said for taking the time now to smell the roses. After all, you won't be able to smell them at your own funeral.

" There is more to life than increasing its speed."

~ Mahatma Gandhi

Watch that bottom line.

What's in your investment portfolio? I'm not referring to cash or other financial assets, but your *life* investments. Education, experiences, friends, interests. Are they delivering the returns you projected? Do you need to perform some asset reallocation, investing a little more in some areas and less in others?

Just as with money, creating and sustaining profitable life investments is a continuing challenge. With money, you know you can't stuff all your cash under a mattress and realistically expect to outperform the market over the long run. Maybe you turn your financial assets over to a money manager, broker, banker, or other professional. Perhaps you educate yourself, gain as much knowledge as you can, and steer the ship on your own with periodic tune-ups by financial experts. Maybe you really do stuff it all in a mattress or shoebox.

You have your hands equally full with your life portfolio. You must take control of your assets, seek continuing education, and continue growing. Perhaps your life portfolio is currently 40% friends, 15% family, 20% school, 10% self-growth, 15% cash reserve (i.e. down time for yourself). That will fluctuate and change over time. Perhaps consciously, maybe because of daily life. Monitoring it, taking control, steering your ship, making decisions based on where you want to go, who you wish to be, and what you want to achieve will all affect your portfolio mix. As example, it can't be 25% hanging out, 5% art, 40% video games, and 30% surfing the 'net, if your desire is to hone your craft as a sculptor. That mix will have to change to create time necessary to further your artistic skill and capabilities.

Make time every six months and assess your life investments. Are you spending (time) wisely? Are you making progress towards important goals? It's a fluid strategy. It's your life. Get the most out of it.

" ... *Investing in yourself is the best thing you can do. Anything that improves your own talents; nobody can tax it or take it away from you.*"

~ Warren Buffett

You're richer than you think.

When you think "lucrative" do you think money? A new business opportunity? A can't miss financial prospect? Most of us do.

Let's take a moment to measure the word from other perspectives. For example, traveling to an exotic destination could be considered lucrative. Learning a new language or a craft is lucrative in its own right. As a culture, we've come to associate so many words with currency or financial status that we overlook other possibilities. Lucrative. Set for life. Wealth. Perhaps financial freedom is the one term associated with money that aptly fits this category. Financial freedom can mean that you see things other than money as having a higher importance. In fact, if you want to feel rich, count all the things you cherish that money cannot buy.

If you read Maslow's hierarchy of needs, you'll discover that once basics are met (food, clothing, shelter), the remainder emphasize friendship, family, self-esteem, respect, confidence, and intimacy; cresting with self-actualization, creativity, spontaneity, morality, and–not surprisingly–acceptance of facts. None having anything to do with money, but all quite lucrative. A word most of us should consider as often as lucrative is *priorities*. Once you've established what is important to you–what has priority in your life, you'll also know what is lucrative to you and how it impacts those priorities.

> "*The key is not to prioritize what's on your schedule, but to schedule your priorities.*"
>
> ~ Stephen Covey

Attention, everyone.

In the area where I live there are a lot of grocers, cafes, restaurants, roadside stands, and food trucks to choose from. Aromatic, scintillating, and tempting; offering my taste buds Thai, American, Mexican, Chinese, Filipino, Hawaiian, Fusion, Japanese, Cajun, Ethiopian, Vietnamese, Korean, Soul, and mash-ups galore. But if I am not hungry, those places don't earn so much as a sniff. However, when I *am* hungry, they become the focus of my attention.

Whatever has a chokehold on your attention controls your motivation and priorities. If your goal is to be the world's most respected neurosurgeon, that's a life priority you'd be highly-motivated to achieve. Even so, if your mind is presently focused on a recently failed investment strategy, paying off your student loan, and fighting to stave off home foreclosure, I'd as soon it not be while you are operating on my brain. These things do not need to share the same time and place.

When your priorities change, your motivation changes, and what gets your attention changes. In life, staying hungry guards you from being slowly eaten from the inside out. So, what grabs your attention? What piques your interest or excites you? What are you hungry for? The only person hunger answers to is the one that feeds it. Stay hungry, my friends.

"Tell me you're never going to die and I won't believe you. Tell me you are going to live and I'll challenge you to prove it."

~ Michael

Let's melt some crayons!

Life isn't lived in black and white. There's a rainbow of colors—some bright, some subdued, and myriad blends in between.

In 1903, the original Crayola colors were black, green, blue, orange, brown, yellow, red, and violet. Well times have evolved (not simply changed, but evolved). As this is written, including both new and retired colors, there have been 133 distinct Crayola colors.

Do you have a favorite? Do some colors create specific feelings or memories for you? Akin to hearing a song that takes you back to a different time in life? Or specific smells—burning leaves, fresh cut grass, a campfire?

Colors and variations come and go, while others hang around as perennial favorites. Many have historical significance or human interest stories associated with them. For instance, priests wear black cassocks in part because it symbolizes a priest dying to self and acts as a reminder that he does not belong to himself, but his bride, the Church. Similarly, the white roman collar is a symbol that they give their lives to Christ and represents the marriage "ring" to the Church.

Have you noticed how few blue foods there are? While blue is one of the most frequently named "favorite" colors, it is one of the least represented (and least appetizing) in the food world. Food researchers say that when humans were primarily hunter-gatherers, they learned to avoid toxic or spoiled objects, which were often blue, purple, or black. They also found that when food is dyed blue, people tend to lose their appetite and eat less than usual. Conversely, Green, red, and brown are the most popular food colors. Savvy restaurant designers often use red decorating schemes because the color red is a proven appetite stimulant. (Wendy's, McDonalds, Burger King, Denny's, Sonic, KFC, Pizza Hut, and Arby's to name a few.)

What color(s) resonate with you? Your least favorite colors are as telling as your favorites. What colors do you identify with? Black = somber? Purple = fun? Is it a combination of both or are they complete opposites? As a teenager, I painted my bedroom black. I liked it. I was a happy guy. My parents hated it. Deep down, I probably just did it for the attention.

There's a tendency to judge people on things as diverse as their tastes in decorating, color, music, cars, and language. ("Extroverts are drawn to bright, outgoing colors like purple, red, yellow, or orange.") Be cognizant of the image you project, but don't be afraid to be yourself. If your color is "grunge rock" so be it. If your color is country, jazz, pop, urban, or swing–so be it.

Things are rarely black or white. If you blend primary colors, you get another. Using all the crayons in your box means achieving an outcome that is uniquely you. You'll break some of those little wax sticks, hate some, and wear others down to a nub. Fantastic! And along the way, remember to share a few of your crayons to others.

"I give bird songs to those who dwell in cities and have never heard them, make rhythms for those who know only military marches or jazz, and paint colors for those who see none."

~ Olivier Messiaen

Extraordinary simply means extra-ordinary.

It may be pronounced differently but extraordinary, is still extra-ordinary. It's from the Latin *extraordinarius*, meaning *extra ordinem*, "outside the normal course of events." The common dictionary meaning is *"beyond what is usual, ordinary, regular, or established."* Hell with that. I'll go down swinging that it does not automatically mean "better" or "fantastic."

Is ordinary, oops, *extra*ordinary your goal? To not only be like everyone else but to be extraordinarily like everyone else? Join me in scrapping the word "extra-ordinary." Seek the astonishing. The challenging. The amazing.

Following are some positive, constructive words. Take a read and see how they could impact your life. And no, they are not listed alphabetically. That would be ordinary.

Nostalgic

"A wistful desire to return in thought or in fact to a former time in one's life; a sentimental yearning for the happiness of a former place or time."

Remember those heart fluttering, topsy-turvy early days of a new relationship? Take a few seconds every day and think about how you can recreate them today. People assume that things can never be as they were in the "early days." That assumption has perpetuated and we take it as "just the way it is." There have been hundreds of books and thousands of articles, blogs, and seminars on "rekindling the flame." What I am curious about, is how the fire was extinguished in the first place. Sure, relationships continually grow, evolve, and change. But we have say in which direction those changes take. There will be disagreements and hardships and challenges. But what if through it all, you strive to maintain that heart fluttering, joyous feeling? Just as you probably have favorite songs from years ago that continue to bring you warming thoughts and comfy feelings, strive to make it so with your life relationship memories.

Adoration

"Reverent and devoted love."

Aaah. Those feelings when you simply look across the room and that wonderful tingle embraces you. This works hand in hand with *nostalgic*. Adoring your partner is an ongoing mission. When your partner and you are in your golden years, and someone were to ask: "Do you remember your first true love?" What greater joy could you have than pointing and replying "Yes, she's sitting right there." So go ahead–point!

Different

"Not alike in character or quality; distinct. Not ordinary; unusual."

Be different. One of a kind. There's much to be said for being you. As we chatted about just a few paragraphs ago–*not* extraordinary. Ralph Waldo Emerson put it succinctly: "To be yourself in a world that is constantly trying to make you something else is the greatest accomplishment."

Attention

"Observant care and consideration. Notice and awareness."

Attention. The thing we crave throughout life. From a crying infant to a screaming toddler tugging on a pant leg, to a pierced-laden teen, to a Maserati driving adult. Attention. We may hide it or mask its allure or pretend it's juvenile. But at the end of the day, we all want to be special. To be someone's homecoming king or queen.

Affection

"Fond attachment, devotion, or love; the emotional realm of love."

This goes hand in hand with attention. Attention may not always be positive or intimate, but when coupled with affection ... a powerful potion. As Jane Austen wrote in *Pride and Prejudice* back in 1813, "Oh Lizzy! Do anything rather than marry without affection."

Courteous

"Having or showing good manners; polite"

As children, we were taught to treat others as we want to be treated. Extended into adulthood, a good analogy might be treating secretaries with as much respect as one would the company president. By far the best example I can think of is, "You can easily judge the character of others by how they treat those who can do nothing for them or to them." (*The Sayings of Chairman Malcolm*).

Even so, many treat the people they care about the most as the least significant. You go on a job interview and you chat up the receptionist, schmooze the HR representative, try to convince the hiring manager that you are the perfect fit, then... go home, toss your car keys on the counter and buzz past your partner to shed your interview suit saying something along the lines of, "Be out in a while, gotta change."

Okay, it's been a challenging day. You want to change clothes, unwind, and relax from a stressful interview (or meeting, or whatever). It only takes a few seconds to pause, greet your partner, and genuinely and sincerely say, "Hi honey. Long day. I missed you. Can't wait to tell you about the interview, give me five minutes." The little things add up to the big things.

Necessary

"Being essential, indispensable, or requisite: a necessary part."

Are you indispensable? Are you the person that he misses with all his heart when you are away? It's easy to become just another part of life, like getting your car repaired or going to the dentist. Neither of which is particularly exciting. Sure, it's "necessary," but *not* the kind of necessary you want to be. Cemeteries are filled with irreplaceable people. By being a necessary partner, you'll always be unforgettable and irreplaceable in your own way.

Important

"Of much or great significance or consequence; entitled to more than ordinary consideration or notice."

How does someone become important in your life? How do you become important in theirs? How will you know when that change happens? What does that feel like? How do you keep it? Sometimes we let trivial stuff get in the way of things that really are important. As American fashion designer and film director Tom Ford said, "From the time we're born until we die, we're kept busy with artificial stuff that isn't important." What will you do to make sure that other person knows the importance they hold in your life?

Priceless

"Having a value beyond all price; invaluable."

Here's a delightful definition: "The most valuable or attractive thing in a collection or group. A prized asset." That reference is to the United Kingdom's Crown Jewels, but I contend it should also apply in your life.

Treasured

"Anything or person greatly valued or highly prized; to regard or treat as precious; cherish."

How is being treasured different from feeling important or necessary? It's a stronger, more intimate feeling of love than "importance." To treasure someone is to feel deep within your heart the value and precious significance they hold in your life.

Beautiful

"Having qualities that give great pleasure or satisfaction to see, hear, think about. Wonderful; very pleasing or satisfying."

Who doesn't love this word? And love to hear it? "You are so *beautiful*." "You make that dress (shirt, etc.) *beautiful* just by wearing it."

Unlimited

"Not limited; unrestricted; unconfined. Boundless; infinite; vast: the unlimited skies. Without any qualification or exception; unconditional."

Saved the best for last. Just re-read the definition. Live your life with unlimited love and attention to those important to you.

See the word similarities? Find the common denominators as they apply in your life. Nostalgic, adoration, attention, different, affection, courteous, necessary, important, priceless, treasured, and unlimited. Common denominator? I bet you already know.

On the other hand, following are a couple of words we all struggle with from time to time:

Criticism

"The act of passing judgment as to the merits of anything. The act of passing severe judgment; censure; faultfinding."

Yes, there is value in criticism. Just keep it positive. You're going to have disagreements and differences of opinion. No one will ever do things exactly as you do. Deal with it. It doesn't make you right or the other person wrong. Finding ways to express criticism in a non-threatening, positive manner is a principal tool for mutually effective communication.

As example, even if you disagree entirely with the way someone is doing something, how about beginning the interaction with "I can tell this is really important to you"? Each of us copes with criticism in our own way. Many of us even welcome *constructive* criticism.

The last thing you should do is to bluntly say things like "You eat with your mouth open. You talk too loud on the phone. You adjust yourself in public." Might be true, but use some diplomacy. Your words will run through their head over and again each time you make a frank observation. Think twice. Talk once. Two ears, one mouth. No coincidence.

Tepid

"Moderately warm; lukewarm. Characterized by a lack of force or enthusiasm."

Ouch. Unfortunately, this describes many relationships. Not really in, yet not out. It's human nature to want the best of all worlds. The comfort the familiar with the freedom of discovery. A healthy relationship fosters both and heats it from tepid to hot, strong, and sustaining. Show some interest. You don't have to like book clubs or baseball or cooking or auto racing. But if it's important to your partner, make it important to you. You don't have to actively participate in an activity, but if your partner plays in a softball league, go and watch a game or two. Cheer them on.

That hour or two means a lot. Besides, you may discover a new hobby. Celebrate your differences, together.

"*At approximately 1,200,000 words, Marcel Proust's* In Search of Lost Time *is the longest book ever written. The shortest?* "*Goodbye.*" *And here's hoping you never read it.*"

~ Michael

Know how to use the locks, but keep your doors open.

"You get in return what you give." Let's add this: "Not necessarily from the same person." You may give love, attention, affection, and friendship to someone. And you will get it in return (when, where, and how makes it all the more interesting), just perhaps not from the people you gave it to. That's the power of paying it forward. Of being an open, sincere, loving person. What goes around comes around, just not necessarily from where you originally sent it or expect it. Be open. Be ready for the boomerang. That's when things get interesting.

Nancy Beaumont, an artist in Edmonds, WA, says she believes if you give as if you know you are loved, you will be. "It's not work, it's acknowledgment. If you can love with no expectations, if you are open to joy, friendship and love, then your life is filled with joy, love and friendship."

What you give does come back, but what you give must come from a place of truth. To do so, you have to understand and believe you are capable of being loved, having friendship, and finding joy. Loving unconditionally does not mean being oblivious of red flags and deal breakers and behaving to protect yourself. Nancy adds, "False security is not love, is not joyful. That's the power of knowing you are deserving of love, friendship, and joy."

"Just as like finds like, love finds love. Embrace it. Be open and giving. Accept love with kindness, grace, and spirit."

~ Michael

Play ball!

Last summer, I attended a baseball game (minor league, single A, for baseball fans out there), at a small stadium–2,400 capacity–with maybe 900 people in attendance, including vendors and players. Now, since I am an avid baseball fan, I recognized the level of play for what it was. Ambitious young men looking to prove their worth and keep their eyes on the big prize–the Major Leagues.

For some of the other spectators, it was as much the experience as the game. Kids couldn't tell the difference between a soaring Babe Ruthian launch and the local 19 year-old's infield pop-up. Nor did it matter. Adults didn't care because they were enjoying the experience. Begs the question–is it the quality or the availability? This also brings into question how to define "the best of" something.

Often, things of high-quality are hard to find, expensive, or both. That's the law of supply and demand. But that applies only to those lagging behind. The followers led down a trodden path behind a visionary or seeker. Go your own way and you might find both quality and availability all by yourself. After all, The Beatles were around and playing long before they were *The Beatles*.

There's joy out there if you want it. Using the baseball example, is watching the Yankees more fulfilling than watching a minor league game? There's arguments both ways (thus proving the point). Is it about the level of play or is it about the experience? Certainly, attending a game of your favorite major league team is a memorable experience. But does that make a minor league or a little league game less enjoyable? If it's about the experience–a game, peanuts, mascot antics, people watching, etc.—you can get it at any local game. Whether you find it in a $100 ticket and a $10 beverage or a $5 ticket and a $2 beverage—the experience is there.

There's a tendency to gauge the depth or satisfaction of an experience based on other people's perceptions. Certainly saying you went to a <insert your favorite artist> concert carries more friend weight and street cred than saying you went to a show at a neighborhood rec center. But does the experience lessen if the people you tell it about don't recognize the artist? Is it about the experience or about impressing others? Enjoy life with others, live life for you.

"Even if you are the only one that does what you do, not everyone is going to care. First and foremost, do it because you care."

~ Michael

In or out, it's your box.

For years we've been inundated with the "think *outside* the box" mantra. How about a little *inside* the box thinking? We often try to craft how we want others to view us, and do so at the expense of who we are. We think externally. What will they think of me? How should I act? What do they expect?

External thinking is like getting in line at the grocery store with an empty cart. You have to know what's inside your cart before someone can ring you up. Try thinking *internally*. Fill that cart with lots of different boxes. No one says you have to fit into any one of them at any given time. Don't label the boxes. Different boxes, different sizes, different days—all bringing new discoveries. Doesn't matter what's in them so long as you do the loading. And when it's your turn to check out, make sure they are all full.

At the end of the day, *spending* time trying to be someone you aren't is mentally exhausting, a waste of good energy, and most people will eventually see through your ruse anyway (likely sooner than later). Instead, *invest* that time in yourself. Ask yourself, "Do I want to live my life trying to gain someone's acceptance at the expense of who I am?" Let me answer for you: No!

"The insurance industry communicates through codes and check-off boxes. If there's no check-off box for you, you don't exist."
~ Jack Anderson, Pulitzer Prize winning reporter

Grasp the gavel. Make your decisions.

Mental Hijacking. A seldom-used term conveying an exceptional concept. Being mentally hijacked means you surrender your personal beliefs to the outside viewpoints of others; blindly assuming that they know what is better for you than you do. And in some cases, they might. Your physician likely knows more about medicine than you do and is better able to know the appropriate treatment for a given ailment. I doubt though that that qualifies her to insist that you drive a Ford and never a Buick. Soliciting opinions and gathering information is valuable. Just be the one sitting at the head of the table come decision time. You, not *they*, live with the consequences.

Ah, "they." An ominous four letter word. Many entanglements begin with the unknown and unnamed *they*. It's the definitive finger-pointing catch-all. The deep-throat of unsubstantiated rumors and hypotheses. "They said ..." "They told me that ..." It's like those mysterious journalistic sources, "uncorroborated," and "confirmed by an unnamed person not authorized to speak to the media."

"They" start a ton of misunderstandings. It's wise not to accept "they" as fact unless "they" have actual names and stand behind their statements. Get the facts, get the names, or ignore "them." Positive things seldom come from unnamed sources.

"They" can be anyone in your life. *They* may be right or wrong. *They* may not have full knowledge of your situation. *They* may be jealous or try to project their situation onto you. *They* may offer good advice. *They* may offer severe, damaging advice. That's why, at the end of the day, *you* must make the decisions. Gather available information, input, and advice, run it through your mental processing grinder, and pull the trigger. Don't become mentally hijacked into believing that the way someone else does something is the only way it can be done. Perform your due diligence then execute the best you can with the information and tools you have.

Use your brain, grasshopper. It's *your* life.

"The most terrifying thing is to accept oneself completely."

~ C.G. Jung

If not for you, you wouldn't be here.

It only takes one person to create change in your life. Who? Go ahead, guess. Yup, you. And you can put that ability to use at it any time. It begins with your thoughts. If you allow negativity and self-doubt to control your thoughts, you'll develop a poor sense of self-worth or low self-esteem. That, in turn, will flow into all the nooks and crannies of your life. It's during those times when you are feeling out of control, trapped, or sliding down a hill without end, that you must tell yourself that *you* control how the story will play out. In any given scenario, *you* have the option to say, "This is not how this story will end." Grab a branch, stop your slide, stabilize, and then continue your climb.

Sure, there are thousands of "just pick yourself up" declarations out there. But they are all meaningless if you don't *do something*. It doesn't matter if you have a hundred self-affirmations taped to your bathroom mirror. Words alone won't really help change how things are going in your life. They might motivate you, short term. They might give you reassurance and get you off the sidelines for a play or two. But the actual work is up to you.

At some point, action is needed. And it's all up to you. You deserve it, but like many things worth having, you have to work for it. It takes resiliency and persistence. Let's use houseplants as an example. You water them, feed them, and prune them. You make sure they get plenty of sunlight, perhaps even talk to them, yet the damn things have the nerve to die anyway. Just goes to show that you can't save the world. Thankfully there's a seed catalog in your mailbox and a nursery just around the corner. Do the best you can, bring joy to the plants in your life, recognize that life is fleeting, and the sooner you get off your rear, the sooner you'll grow the life you're looking for.

Oh, and spoiler alert—you'll have to deal with a lot of fertilizer along your journey. Compost heaps are filled with irreplaceable plants. Point? Plants die, often regardless of how much love and nourishment you provide. They frequently flourish on a hillside with no attention at all. Others, you might toss aside, come back a few years later and they are everywhere. But since you tossed it aside, I believe that your definition for that plant had changed to "weed." If you take the time to grow it, take a close look before you throw it.

Tell yourself, "I am determined. My path continues. I will persevere and grow stronger with each setback. I'll be a little less fearful with every battle. Each day I will grow more resistant to pain and to attack. I am not fearful of rain, snow, or freezing ice. You can burn me, cut me, but you will not defeat me. I will never give up. I will come back stronger than before. I know no other way. I am the strongest weed in life's garden." Remember too, even these are just words. It's still up to you.

"People tend to overstate my resilience, but, of course, I hope they're right."

~ David Brudnoy

The rings of life.

As dendrochronologists can tell you, dendrochronology is the science of tree-ring dating based on the analysis of tree ring growth patterns. In many types of wood, dendrochronology can pinpoint the time trees were formed with calendar year accuracy. They are, indeed, the rings of life.

While we humans have no such visible rings (save a few wrinkles or scars), most of us can identify with clarity the defining moments in our lives and in the world as we see it. Our rings of life, if you will, form all that we are and all we have been. Rings there for the duration and cannot be altered.

No one and no thing can give you a better past. You can run from it, but can't hide from it. Moreover—you shouldn't. You are a sum of all you have been and experienced. Harnessing that will create all you can become. Some are going to judge you solely on the past anyway. Good or bad; especially in matters of the heart. It's just so damn easy to do. But logically, we know it doesn't always hold water.

In finance, it's "past performance is no guarantee of future returns." In music or arts, "you're only as good as your last hit." And when talking of people, it seems to boil down to making judgments based on yesterday; not the future. Unfortunately, some of us do live down to that reputation and meet those undesirable expectations. But keeping an open heart and an open mind sure frees up a lot of brain power.

I'm not naïve. If someone enters into an agreement, whether personal (marriage) or professional (business partnership), and breaks that trust—there are consequences. But holding an advance expectation that a storm is brewing is asking for trouble. If you enter into marriage assuming your partner will be unfaithful, you will be contributing to a suspicious environment that is not conducive to a loving union (continually checking their whereabouts as example). You might not be directly responsible if something goes upside down, but you were in the arena while the game was being played. You know the saying: Fool me once, shame on you. Fool me twice, shame on me. Add to that; fool me three times, shame on both of us.

Stuff happens. That's what renter, homeowner, life, disability, auto, health, and dental insurance is for. You don't buy a house expecting it to burn down. You make it your home. A tumult-free comfy lair, holding full faith it will never burn to the ground. It might. But if you go to bed every night expecting it to happen, you aren't really enjoying your home. Prepare for the worst–expect the best.

Use some common sense. If you buy a house situated on a cliff in earthquake territory, a downhill sled ride on your roof shouldn't really come as a surprise. Make the best decision you can with the information you have, then trust in yourself, in your decision, and in others. You are going to get burned (no fire pun intended) a time or two. That goes into your mental toolbox. But you cannot judge all future events with a similar expectation or you'll never be happy or content. Don't enter marriage with a "Well, he's going to cheat on me and steal my money, but here goes," attitude. Do you want to buy a house telling yourself, "It's going to go up like a chimney in 46 months, 3 weeks, and 6 days?" No. Even if you possessed that knowledge and could see the future, wouldn't it be better to live that time happily? Have the courage to trust.

So, we're full circle. No one nor any things can give you a better past. And only you can give yourself the bright future you deserve. Use the past to your advantage. All those experiences, mistakes, joys, sorrows, and achievements. All are arrows in your quiver, arming you for what lay around the bend. No, you can't change your past. But you can use it as your springboard. Remember, a bad day is just that: one day. Another learning tool. Extract what you can from it then discard it and move forward. You always get a second chance. It's called tomorrow.

"You learn from the past. You don't live there."

~ Michael

The destination is only one stamp in your life passport.

So, it's supposed to be all about the journey, not the destination. Spoiler alert! It's actually about both. Your journey lasts throughout your lifetime, during which you will reach numerous destinations. And each life destination is both a finishing line and starting point.

Using a martial arts example; when you punch, your arm and fist don't accelerate just to the end of the motion and then stop. Our mind tells us to start decelerating as we *near* the target as to reduce impact. But that's opposite of what we're trying to accomplish (full force impact). To achieve this, you must visualize your target beyond where it actually is. In this manner, you'll still be accelerating on impact. The blow doesn't end it after striking the target (similar to how a golfer continues his follow-through after the clubhead contacts the ball).

So what does this have to do with your journey? In life, it means not stopping when you reach a destination. A destination is a single vista of your life journey. Perhaps where you find your partner, or take the three month cruise you've saved years for. But life continues after the event. And destinations are events. Life memories. Souvenirs. Who you are and become.

Similar to a summer road trip, your journey and discoveries prepare you for your next destination. Once reaching a destination, you've already (even if by auto-pilot) made arrangements to continue. (Fueling or charging the car, checking tires, oil, lights, and all the myriad things needed to keep your vehicle going.) Each destination on your journey also mentally prepares you for the next by replenishing you spiritually, emotionally, teaching you how to overcome obstacles and setbacks, and creating an ever-growing "you" toolbox. Not all things get better *with* age. Some things get better because *we* age. We learn, mature, experience, and earn a healthy appreciation of it all. Keep your foot on the pedal, know when to use the brake, and enjoy the journey and its many destinations along the way. It's all about the adventure.

"I see my path, but I don't know where it leads. Not knowing where I'm going is what inspires me to travel it."

~ Rosalia de Castro

If it's heavy, put it down for a while.

Are you living a sustainable life? I don't mean eating organic or going green. I'm referring to physical and emotional sustainability. For instance; anger, resentment, and fear are not perpetually sustainable. Those feelings happen. They slip in, serve a purpose, and then slide out.

What qualities *do* you desire? Once you can identify those desires, ask yourself—are they sustainable? Do you allow them to be sustainable? Every garden grows, ebbs, and returns fresh. Plant only what you desire, knowing even weeds serve a purpose. If contentment is one of your sustainable goals, you have to be willing to let go of anger and resentment. If good health is a goal, you must include regular exercise as part of your daily habits. No magic wand here. It's relatively straight forward.

Some of your objectives will be easier to measure than others. It can be difficult to gage how much resentment or anger you are carrying around. Sometimes it's obvious and other times it might seem everyone but you notices it. (In fact, your close friends or partner are your best source for valuable feedback.)

You've probably noticed that it's challenging to stay focused on your goals when you're depressed or angry. Those negative emotions (and that's all they are–emotions), fighting you every step of the way, are powerful stumbling blocks.

It's like mentally running the gauntlet. You must remain focused on your end game, absorb the blows, and keep moving forward. If it was *always* easy you wouldn't be reading this book right now. You can't paint a landscape while juggling chainsaws. If contentment is one of your sustainable goals, you'll need to lay down your burdens and focus on doing whatever it is that brings you that peace and contentment.

You can't lug a heavy boulder across the country without resting. We often don't realize how heavy something is until we put it down. It's not putting the boulder down and taking a rest that's quitting. Quitting is not picking the boulder back up.

"Waste your money and you're only out of money, but waste your time and you've lost a part of your life."

~ Michael LeBoeuf

Trivia time.

Who is the only National Basketball Association (NBA) player to
score 100 points in a single game? Michael Jordan? Nope. Kobe
Bryant? Nada. LeBron James? Air ball. Most Consecutive Wins on
the Professional Golfers' Association (PGA) tour? Tiger Woods?
Nope. Jack Nicholas? Nada. Most runs scored in Major League
Baseball (MLB)? Babe Ruth? Nope. Hank Aaron? No. Ty Cobb?
Swing and a miss. (The answers, for non-sports fanatics, are: Wilt
Chamberlain, Byron Nelson, and Rickey Henderson.)

So where's this leading? Simply that sometimes it isn't the
person that first comes to mind that reaches the pinnacle of
success in a chosen endeavor. (Notice, I wrote 'endeavor' and not
'sports.') Make a habit of scratching beneath the surface. Read a
few more pages of a book before you give up on it. Listen to
another track on that album before you decide you can't live with
it or without it (or both).

You'll make numerous discoveries as you meander along your
path. You might not recognize some of those hidden jewels until
you've give them a chance to soak in and can appreciate them for
what they bring to your life. And that's okay too. Treasures are all
around. Keep your eyes (and more important) your mind open. It
comes easier when you accept that you probably won't discover
whatever "it" is in the first book you crack. I like to tell people that
I try to learn something new every day and that every day I learn
how little I know. Just don't give up. Keep hunting and keep
discovering. Consider ...

Pete Rose is MLB's all-time hits leader (4,256 for those scoring
at home). It certainly wasn't by chance as he is also the all-time

leader in number of at bats. And of those 4,000+ hits, is another telling record. Most singles. Yup, he did it one base at a time. Persistence, determination, and a will not only to put on the uniform but to be the best. Failure is part of that journey. In fact he hit only 160 home runs during his 24 year career in nearly 16,000 plate appearances while striking out more than 1,100 times. His nickname? "Charlie Hustle."

"Nothing motivates me more than the sound of a ticking clock, snapping off my life in one second increments."

~ Michael

A *real* icebreaker for you.

Some people (not you or me, naturally!) tend to initially size others up as they would an iceberg: by what's visible. Just as it's common to judge on the three minute dance, not the thousands of hours devoted to practice. Never mind the sweat, study, and sacrifice. And contrary to the popular saying of "practice makes perfect"–no, it doesn't. Perfection is an elusive, meandering figment of imagination. If only I would have. I should have. Or if I lost five lbs. or had a nose job, or studied until 3am instead of going to bed at 2am … There will always be a big "if" and there will never be a resounding "perfect." Sure you can throw a perfect game in baseball or get a perfect score in gymnastics. But no *person* is perfect.

You can't just skip practice and go straight to opening night. (We listen to Bach for hours, loving the sound, tempo, and brilliant arrangements without consideration for the endless hours of practice and study, years of struggle, and unwavering dedication and belief.) All you can do is be your best you. Put in the time. And don't be your own worst enemy. There'll be plenty of others looking to fill that role. Jealousy, people too afraid to try, people not putting in the time and resenting you for getting the accolades.

Find individuals that can best appreciate your effort and results. Those who recognize and understand the work required. Peer recognition is significant because they know and understand the related dedication. It's a principal reason why study groups, clubs, and industry associations are so useful. No one understands a chemist better than a chemist. Likewise you might appreciate the beauty of a Bach composition, but having an understanding of what went into the creation brings a whole new level of appreciation for both the composer and the work.

Now, about that iceberg. Typically, only about ten percent of the total bulk of an iceberg is visible above the waterline. The underwater portion of a berg can be difficult to gauge simply by looking at the portion poking through the surface. Thus the expression, "That's just the tip of the iceberg." Kind of a big deal when you consider that the largest known iceberg was approximately 551 ft. above sea level (reported by the USCG icebreaker *East Wind* in 1958), making the overall height similar to that of a 55-story building.

Learning to appreciate the entire iceberg, not just the bit pushing above the surface is fundamental in appreciating the incredible pieces of nature they are. Just as we humans are all individual, deep creatures. What you see is only part of what you get.

Take time to get to know the entire person. Find out what's beneath the surface. Even if you can move heaven and earth for someone, you'll still uncover worms and mud. No one's perfect. (And, you'll get your feet dirty.) Go about living your life and do your best for yourself whether others see it and recognize it or not.

"The reality of the other person is not in what he reveals to you, but in what he cannot reveal to you. Therefore, listen not to what he says but rather what he does not say."

~ Kahlil Gibran

Desperate times, desperate measures.

People frequently associate *desperation* with dating. With finding, attracting, and keeping a partner. We talk about appearing desperate and how to avoid it. But romance doesn't have a stranglehold on desperation. It can pop its head up anywhere. Job search, paying bills, and friendship issues to name a few.

Consider a scenario that finds you two months behind on your car payment with no other means of transportation, living in a rural area fifteen miles from town and your job, with no bus transport or other way to commute. You need your next paycheck to catch up the car payment, but won't get it till a week from Friday. Driving will likely result in your car being repossessed while you are at work. However you choose to resolve this will entail a bit of desperation. Decisions made in desperation are typically rash, impulsive, and at odds with those you'd otherwise make. You need immediate resolution to solve a challenge.

Things are easier when you can play from a position of strength, like looking for a job when you don't need one or having your car serviced regularly so it doesn't break down. Use foresight, but have a plan B and a plan C. Desperation should always be plan Z (but have a plan for it!). You can't plan for your parachute to not open but you can plan for what to do if it doesn't. Life happens. Like Benny Hill stated, "Just because nobody complains doesn't mean all parachutes are perfect."

You prepare during the calm, knowing there'll be a storm, so that you can prosper in its aftermath. In the car example, having learned to ride a bike will help you get to work and earn the paycheck you need for the past due car payment. And after that storm has passed, you can prosper having ridden the bicycle to and from work. Better health, cash in hand, and maybe you'll discover joy in riding the bike.

Desperate times, desperate measures. Survival. You do what you have to do. Determination triumphs desperation. Just don't lose the lesson. Like the mythical Phoenix, rise from the ashes of desperation stronger, more aware, more vibrant, and wiser than ever. This too shall pass.

"Desperation is sometimes as powerful an inspirer as genius."

~ Benjamin Disraeli

Who's fooling whom?

There's an old adage that states, "Fool me once shame on you. Fool me twice, shame on me." The only thing that really says is that you didn't learn from the first experience, and, since you didn't get what you wanted the first time, you won't bother trying again.

In an ideal world, we learn lessons once and we never repeat mistakes. In the real world, life is a continuous succession of tweaks and adjustments. We often need to learn a lesson more than once ... or twice. Sometimes we have to repeat the lesson to deepen our understanding, adjust our sails, and incorporate new learning and findings. So, sure—if you screw me over twice, I deserve to point the finger at myself. But, the real finger pointing begins when you are fooled for the same reason without making the necessary adjustments.

If you stick your hand in fire, I bet you won't intentionally do it again. But you probably won't shy away from it either. You'll make adjustments: hands clear, no dangling clothing, no dry wood or leaves near the campsite, no open burning during dry season. One lesson learned many times, refining your results each time. Only when you disregard the lesson is it futile. Everything for a reason.

"Mostly, we should remember those things we try to forget. Things forgotten take their lessons with them. Memorize the lesson."

~ Michael

A hole in one!

To borrow a bit of corporate personnel review vernacular, we all have "areas for improvement." You'll never be all things to all people, and you'll make more progress by developing and playing to your strengths than you will by focusing your energy on eliminating weaknesses. One is a by-product of the other. Ignore your strengths and they'll atrophy till they are no more than a weakness. As Mark Twain said about literacy, "The man who does not read has no advantage over the man who cannot read."

By developing your strengths, weaknesses ebb on their own. The caveat here is what many define as fatal flaws: those things that hinder the development of your inherent strengths. These might include poor reading skills for a teacher or weak math ability for a budding scientist. Those fall under that ominous "areas for improvement" umbrella, and must be addressed in unison with the ongoing development of your core strengths.

You'll also do well to remember this: As you hone your strengths, it's essential to use them to advantage. As example, if you enjoy playing the links and have earned a 3 handicap, don't get duped into playing a game of mini-golf to decide who buys dinner.

"Have enough sense to know, ahead of time, when your skills will not extend to wallpapering."

~ Marilyn vos Savant

Read, write, or get out of the way.

When you've got a job waiting, having the appropriate tools available is mighty handy. But even the highest-quality tools are simply the means to an end; you still have to do the heavy lifting. As example, writing a 500 page novel may be physically faster and easier on the hands using a keyboard than with an inkwell, quill, and parchment, but the brain and thought energy requirement is not lessened. It appears easier because—let's face it—we progressed from scratching out errors with a quill to ripping paper from a typewriter and starting anew, to using correction ribbon, to liquid paper, to a simple backspace or cut and paste function. With voice recognition software, even simpler. But the thought process, the creative spark, the idea and its expression remains unchanged. Different path, same result.

If you can't fly, take a train or car. If you don't have a car, ride a bike. No bike? Walk. The tools are available. They may not be the tools you want, but there are options. You can choose not having a computer as an *excuse* to not write, or, you can use paper and pen. Of course, you could also just sit around feeling sorry for yourself and wait for someone to tell you how bad everything is. That choice is available as well. It's up to you.

"The only thing standing between you and your goal is the bullshit story you keep telling yourself as to why you can't achieve it."
~ Jordan Belfort (Author, *The Wolf of Wall Street*)

Oh, you mean now?

If you tell me you want or need something "as soon as possible" (ASAP) that's exactly when you'll get it. Of course, *As Soon As Possible* means something different to a caffeine fueled, Type A personality than it does to someone living on island time.

Be *specific*. ASAP is a gray, ambiguous expression. It's a brewing misunderstanding. "I thought I told you ASAP?!" "You did. And that's exactly when you got it!"

"As *often* as possible" is ASAP's similarly ambiguous cousin. Often is a vague expression, meaning something different to everyone. All this can be avoided by being specific in your requests. If you tell me as soon and as often as possible, that's exactly when you'll get it.

Yet another sterling example of ambiguity is telling someone that something you want is "more important than ever." This can be interpreted as minimizing someone's effort up till then. Saying something is "*as* important as ever," would be more thoughtful.

"Say what you mean and mean what you say." That's some straight-forward, sage advice, but it can present challenges if you aren't really sure of one or the other. Being congruent is essential for achieving common understanding and agreeable results. Sometimes problems occur from something as simple as a person not really knowing what they mean, or, they choose their words poorly and are misinterpreted. Due to this, meaning what you say may be something entirely different than saying what you mean.

Something ambiguous has (at least) two possible interpretations. Though sometimes humorous ("kids make nutritious snacks"), it can also cause exhausting frustration in our personal relationships, turning something innocuous into a frustrating scrum. Here's an example of an insignificant exchange that could easily snowball:

"Do you need a water glass or do you already have one?"

"Yes," he replied.

"Yes, what?" she asked.

"Yes, I do."

"Yes, you do, what?"

"Need a glass."

"Then why didn't you say so?"

"I did!"

Sounds like a cheesy comedy skit, but I can tell you, the person standing in the kitchen with their hand on the cabinet knob didn't find it amusing. Just annoying and frustrating.

Here are some tips on reducing ambiguity:

- Thinking before you speak.
- Asking for clarification ("What I hear is...").
- Consider your response before it comes out of your mouth. If you're texting, emailing, or chatting, take a moment to read your words aloud before hitting send, because once you click that magic button—those words live forever.

As a side note, one thing I try to remember—especially during interviews or when giving presentations—is to insert a pause in my speech from the beginning. As example, when asked my name, I'll give a slight pause before responding. Why? Because when one is asked a difficult question or caught off-guard, the natural tendency is to pause as we determine the best way to respond. By opening the entire exchange with a slight pause, it lessens the appearance of a "gotcha!" moment down the line (and provides opportunity to make sure we say what we mean and mean what we say).

"Courage is what it takes to stand up and speak; courage is also what it takes to sit down and listen."

~ Winston Churchill

It's all here, in black and white.

There are only twenty-six letters in the (English) alphabet, but oh what we say (and write). For monolingual English writers and speakers, those twenty-six letters hold every word you've written and every word you have spoken. Twenty-six little letters that form everything you do and every word that describes you. No matter how unique and indescribable you believe yourself to be, it will not stop people from pasting their own label on you. To others, none of us are undefinable. You're writing your legacy - one letter at a time, one word at a time, one interaction at a time.

Further compounding things, those twenty-six letters can be used to create more than forty distinct sounds, with most of those sounds serving more than one purpose. Naturally, many words have multiple meaning whether spoken or written. And unless you're dealing with someone you know intimately (or perhaps, *especially* then), give some thought to what you say before you say it. Pause before you speak. Think, "What will happen if I say this? What is the potential fallout?" Same goes for those fingers tapping away on your phone or keyboard. Remind yourself to *count to ten before you send.*

Okay. With your written communications, you've re-read your missive for intent and purpose. Now, keep your finger off the 'send' toggle for a few more seconds. Before launching it into hyperspace, consider this little tidbit: Often it's not the wording but the punctuation (or lack thereof) that creates confusion. Love, Michael has an entirely different implication than Love Michael. Or this disturbing example: Time to eat, Grandpa and Time to eat Grandpa. When writing, take time to carefully consider your words and be certain their context clearly denotes your intended meaning. And don't forget to check your spelling and grammar. "Heaven nos most of use have falling victim to a well-meaning spellcheck a time or too." But that's a story for another typo.

P.S. If you really want to exercise your language skills, try Hawaii. The 50th US state's official alphabet consists of just thirteen letters.

"Bad grammar makes me [sic]."
~ Unknown

Well, this is puzzling.

We've been building jigsaw puzzles since London cartographer John Spilsbury began producing them around 1760. For various reasons, they've flustered us since. The boxes don't always contain all the pieces, the factory messes up, you lose a piece, or maybe someone hides a piece or two (you know who you are).

You can't just dump the box and expect the pieces to magically put themselves together. You assemble the easy pieces, then it's up to you to jigsaw the rest. Much like life, isn't it? We'd like everything to fall into place and look like the picture in our head without having to make any effort. While that would be convenient, it sure would take away most of why we're here in the first place. (You don't want a cookie cutter life do you?)

You can manipulate those interlocking mysteries, turn the whole thing upside down, flip it sideways, take scissors to the disagreeable pieces that are *obviously* mis-cast, push, squint, squeeze, press, threaten, toss it to the floor and start over, or ask for help. Wait. Here's another idea. Sweep the entire cookie cutter box aside and make your own jigsaw puzzle. It's your vision, it's your puzzle. Maybe it won't look like other people think it should, but the pieces will form. Give yourself benefit of the doubt. It's entirely up to you—either way, the puzzle always completes. And when it takes shape to your liking, give it its proper name. *Life.*

~ Know what's worse than losing? Not playing. ~

Personally, I like peanut butter.

Do you make time to think about yourself, for yourself? To take both a macro and micro personal assessment, drilling down to your core being; all of your life's nooks and all of its crannies? Do you take the time to ask yourself: regardless of current trends, fads, or easily accessible bandwagons, "Does this make sense to *me*? Does this make sense *for* me? Does it pass my smell test?"

Independent thinking is a key attribute for living a fulfilling life. Sure, you'll hit a few clunkers, have some undesirable outcomes, and make a few unfortunate decisions. So what. When you get it wrong, get it wrong for yourself. The finger you point at the mirror is always pointing at the person responsible for your decisions. Think not? If something blows up in your face, nine times out of ten guess who everyone will be staring at? Yup. I'm willing to bet you dinner that if something bad happens you'll hear, "what did you do?" or, "what happened?" long before you hear, "Who told you to do that?" Even if I'm wrong (dinner's on the line!), it makes sense to gather as much information as you can before pulling the trigger on important decisions. If for no other reason than for your own peace of mind. If you don't like peanut butter, don't eat peanut butter cookies just because everyone else is. It doesn't matter if it makes sense if it doesn't make sense for *you*.

"If you choose to put all your eggs into one basket, make sure that

you are the basket."

~ Michael

We all walk the same earth.

You're likely familiar with the phrase, "What's in it for me" (WIIFM). Or, just as likely, "Why should I give a crap?"

In business, most people don't really care how long you took to develop your widget or how great your gizmos are. They likely don't give a rat's butt that your engineers worked 24 hour days, slept on a concrete floor, and survived on cold pizza and caffeine-infused energy drinks. At the end of the day ... "Great story, thanks for sharing, now ... why do I give a crap?"

Marketing 101: features and benefits. Features are *what* it is. For example, you might tell a far-sighted, arthritic person that your gizmo has large numbers and a free-wheeling dial. The benefits are where you make the sale. In that example, you're asking someone to figure it out on their own. If you want the sale, you'd be better served providing the solution–not the equation: "You don't need reading glasses to see the numbers and the dial spins easily so it won't aggravate your arthritis." That speaks directly to the person. You solved a problem by addressing issues important to *them.*

The same principle applies in life. An archetypal example: People love hearing their own name. As Dale Carnegie wrote in his 1936 classic, *How To Win Friends and Influence People,* "A person's name is to that person the sweetest and most important sound in any language." People don't listen much until you've given them a compelling reason and told them how they will benefit. We all chase the WIIFM angle.

Many believe WIIFM is a selfish approach to life. The virtues of selflessness and generosity are carved into us with diamond-like precision at an early age. But it's also true that doing something that brings you no promise of joy or value (whatever *value* means to you), it may not be worthy of your time investment. And that's okay. WIIFM doesn't have to be a narcissist, selfish thing. WIIFM can refer to any number of things. From the obvious, "I'm hungry, I'm going to eat," to much broader situations. Perhaps you choose to help dig a mile-long four feet deep trench. You gain physical health and strength and the satisfaction of helping small farm owners irrigate their crops. If we see WIIFM as a simple, short-term notion (I don't want to dig a hole), we'll struggle to form a broader life perspective.

Take a moment and consider the ramifications. Sometimes helping others *is* WIIFM. Reframing the WIIFM to WIIFU (what's in it for *us*) often creates a greater utilitarian value. Finding and participating in life on common ground enriches everyone. You helped dig a trench, we all ate.

Even Mother Teresa received something in return for her humanitarian efforts—the knowledge that she was making a difference to others. As she famously said, "The hunger for love is much more difficult to remove than the hunger for bread." Mother Teresa recognized that we all have a need, a hunger, to feel and be loved. Just as I recognize that you are not reading this because *I* wrote it. You're reading it because *you* want the message and information.

Go ahead—live with élan. When you are looking to make a connection with someone, remember that they are seeking something just as you are. Discovering common ground will give you a greater understanding of the person and also the knowledge to make a determination on whether it's a path you wish to share. You might also find that you are drawn to a person's dissimilarities. Recognizing those differences as learning opportunities for personal (and partnership) growth comes with much value as well.

In all, forging your own path means passing lots of side trails and byways. Along the way, you might just come across a few people heading the same direction as you with a similar, or intriguing, mission of their own.

~ There is no they. Only us. ~

So, who are you anyway?

Humans are capricious. In the United States, politics are a textbook example. Voters elect candidates into office and then proceed to heckle them through their last day of service. It often seems that giving people what they (think) they want proves one of two things: they didn't know what they wanted or they didn't know what they were getting. None of America's most popular presidents garnered unanimous approval. History books can be skewered by myriad factors. The personal politics of the person who wrote it, the government behind it, wishful thinking, or well-intended authors. We aim both to please and to be understood. History is rewritten daily and daily history written and recast by the minute.

As humans, we want to be right and desirable. But casting your line and expecting everyone to admire you can make for frustrating times. Besides, giving others what they want won't necessarily provide others with what they need. You need to unselfishly put your own life at the top of your list. After all, how can you possibly expect to be valuable to another without first knowing what you are all about? Work your life from the inside out. Find and follow your path. If you change "beliefs" every time you meet someone you (think you) want to impress, you'll never get anywhere.

"If one morning I walked on top of the water across the Potomac River, the headline that afternoon would read 'President Can't Swim'."

~ Lyndon B. Johnson

Relax, already.

The early bird gets the worm, but that's not much of an advantage if you don't like worms. You don't have to run a race because everyone else is running. You don't have to be the first person on the plane (the tail section arrives [fingers crossed] at the same time as the nose). Sure, some things do require a sense of urgency, but along the way there's nothing wrong with scheduling some downtime for yourself. What good is something if you don't experience it in a manner that relates to your senses? You were the last one in the pool? So what. The pool wasn't going anywhere. You may have sucked in a little more urine than the first jumper, but otherwise, no difference. Save the urgent times for urgent things. Living at 100 MPH 24/7 doesn't leave much time to savor what you're working so hard for.

Job, family demands, the self-imposed guilt. The phone, TV, traffic noises, and, unfortunately, sometimes the incessant cackling of others. You have to fight for your all-important "me" time. Give yourself permission to be selfish. Spend some time alone. Recognize and respect when it's time to take your foot off the gas pedal and set your inner-cruise control to "idle." From time to time doing nothing is an achievement in itself. After all, being overwhelmed can, at times, be more unproductive than doing nothing.

"Doing nothing is better than being busy doing nothing."

~ Lao Tzu

We'll wait and see what happens.

Are you a planner or more of a spontaneous person? It's possible that you might be both. As example, if you set aside a block of time—an hour, a day, a week—for yourself, to do whatever you want, you have *planned* to be spontaneous. Some people have a hard time letting go of their preplanned, rigorous schedules and being spontaneous just doesn't *feel right* for them. But it is possible to be a spontaneous planner.

Let's use a NASA launch as example. What happens during the ten second countdown? Does everyone stand around waiting for a ginormous poof of smoke and the earth-shaking rumble of the blast-off? Of course not. The short clip we see on the news—the "spontaneous launch"—is the culmination of years of meticulous planning and work.

You can't just blink, nod your head, or snap your fingers and expect something magical to happen. Nor can you count it down and expect positive results without first planning then taking steps to achieve your desired "lift-off."

The larger your desires, the more thought you'll need to put into the planning and execution. For instance, you might be able to raze a small ranch home or a barn in a day or two using a bulldozer and the help of a few willing assistants. But if you're planning to implode a 40 story building, you'll need to do more than screech up in a truck, fling on a hard hat, and count to three. Demolition experts put in countless hours planning, calculating, and running through myriad hypotheses before they press the magic button.

Those are extreme examples, but the logic holds true in everyday life. Even when your plan is to plan *nothing*. Even living a random life of a nomad without any sense of what you are looking to achieve requires both a plan and a subsequent action.

It is possible to have a life focused on happiness, relationships, and a fulfilling profession (all which require effort to attain a modicum of perceived success), and still be okay with planning not to plan. We all need our downtime. If your plan for Tuesday and Sunday of the third week of next August is to do nothing, you've still essentially made a plan. In essence: Make sure to plan for time that isn't planned.

"*Sometimes, doing nothing* is *doing something.*"

~ Michael

"I want to be rich!"

Okay, fine. You want to be rich. First, you'll need to define what being rich means to you. Is it money? Health? A loving relationship? Super powers? The admiration of friends and family? None of those? All of them? As individuals, we place distinct values on various aspects of life and love and the wealth it gives us. Some people might say loving relationships with their children and family while others would say having more money than Scrooge McDuck (or dare I say ... Bill Gates). This individuality is part of what makes us who we are and helps define our personal wealth.

What are your wildest dreams? Those things that wake you in the night. The pulling. The tugging. Your daydreams. In the back of your mind, there is usually something mulling around. Dangling. Sitting there waiting for your discovery and acceptance. And it probably isn't just one thing. What are they and, most important, *do you have a plan* to achieve them or are they still dreams? Taking action on your dreams is what makes you rich–however you choose to define it.

"There is a gigantic difference between earning a great deal of money and being rich."

~ Marlene Dietrich

Happiness is an extreme emotion.

Happiness is no more a sustainable way of life than fear or sadness or sorrow. Do this: draw a horizontal line. Now draw a horizontal line above it and another below it. Label the top line, "elated" and the bottom line, "miserable." Now consider your present life. It's a fluctuating compromise between happy and miserable. We can't realistically expect to be elated 100% of the time, nor do any of us want to be miserable all the time. The challenge is to recognize and cherish those elated times. Likewise, sad moments need not dominate our lives. Both happiness and sadness are extreme emotions.

Life happens. Your challenge is to recognize the extremes, know that they will come, and navigate towards that first horizontal line you drew. That middle line that we shall label *contentment*.

"*The world is full of people looking for spectacular happiness while they snub contentment.*"

~ Doug Larson

This is my bed. Find your own!

Don't complicate your life–it will do that on its own. If you continually think about the "I should, I could, my tooth hurts, I have a bruise" ... you'll forever swim in a pool of self-imposed misery. What if you instead choose to focus on things that build happiness and bring you joy? Don't feed life's negative fires; they too can do that on their own. Learn to control the spread, extinguish what you can, and get safely away from the rest. Yes, it's much easier said than done. (I've spent my share of nights lying awake mulling life, health, mortality, or financial issues.)

I learned the hard way (don't we all) that you need to put that stuff to bed the same time as you, but *not* in the same bed. Go to bed focusing on something positive in your life (or that you want in your life). Maybe you imagine giving an important speech, or being in a musical, or being a pro athlete. Think about living the life you imagine. Doesn't matter that you may not have done it (yet)–they are your dreams. No one can take away what you keep in your mind. And remember too, dreams aren't just for the sleeping hours. There's a little bit of Walter Mitty in all of us.

" The quieter you are, the louder you hear."

~ Michael

Home sweet home.

I love the notion of dropping everything (though few of us leave their tablet, laptop, or phone at home) and going on vacation to do things that we don't otherwise do. But couldn't we consider life a continuing vacation by doing what we love to do and living the life we want to live every day? Seem naïve? Not how the "real world" works? Fair enough. Perhaps we can chat after you spend fifty weeks doing something you loathe so that you can have a week or two to do something you enjoy.* I know, I know. You'll do what you really want to with your life when you retire, because that's what society has programmed you to do. (To those of you loving your vocation because it's as much a part of you as breathing, go ahead and skip a few paragraphs to the part where you should be loving it in your dream locale.)

For a taste of this, U.S. readers simply need to turn on a television and check out the barrage of ads that typically start around March each year—the time school spring break traditionally begins and when people begin planning their annual "vacation." The ads are quick to point out everything you are missing. If you live in an Arizona desert community, why, you could be sailing, surfing, and swimming in San Diego. If you live in San Francisco, you'll learn that you need to be in Los Angeles for the theme parks and movie lot tours. If you live in Los Angeles, you'll be told that you should be sitting by a crackling fire in the Washington State wilderness, or hiking Mount Rainier. If you live in Iowa, you should be in New York. Live in New York? Why aren't you in Florida working on your beach tan? If you're in Miami, why aren't you getting rum soaked in the Keys? In the Keys? Why aren't you in New York City taking in Time Square?

No matter where you are, marketers happily point out that you should be someplace else. You know, for "vacation." For some unknown reason, we aren't supposed to live in the places that bring us great joy, only visit them for 2–3 % of our life. Makes sense, right? I thought not. You might think I'm missing the point in that vacations enable us to experience other places. That our personal utopia would become ordinary if we lived there. Perhaps. Then how about this for compromise: Live where you want and do what you want in surroundings you dream of. Spend that other 2-3% a year seeing something else, rather than the other way round.

You might be thinking, "That's easy for him to say—he doesn't have to get up and go to my crappy job just to pay for this shitty car and apartment. That's the way life works, pal." My response would be—short of being held at gunpoint—you applied for that job, bought that car, and you selected that apartment. And, if you did so because you needed food, transportation, and a roof, then you'd need the same things *no matter where you were.* You made the choice. The power of that is, you can also make the choice to change it.

This points to the necessity of using your desires to produce goals and creating your desired reality from those goals. You took millions of small steps—consciously or otherwise, desirous or from a perceived necessity—to get to where you are today, this very minute. Think about what and where you *want* to be and take those steps one at a time till you get there.

Few of us can quit our job, pack up our stuff, and move to (our personally defined) exotic locale on a whim. Want to change course? You have the helm. Plot the course and go. It won't happen overnight. Even the fleetest luxury ship must first slow and prepare before executing its turn to a new course. It's the preparation that makes the course change possible.

* *The United States is one of only seven industrialized countries (Micronesia, Tonga, Sri Lanka, Marshall Islands, Palau, Pakistan are the others) that have no statutory minimum employment leave laws.*

"You always do what you want to do. This is true with every act. You may say that you had to do something, or that you were forced to, but actually, whatever you do, you do by choice. Only you have the power to choose for yourself."

~ W. Clement Stone

Sometimes the book belongs back on the shelf.

Even bad books can be hard to put down once you've invested time in them. You get 150 pages into a 400 page tome and realize it just isn't clicking for you. But, because of your time investment, you keep reading. You rationalize that you may as well finish the book even though it sucks, it's bringing you no enjoyment, and you could easily spend time reading books that bring you relaxation, knowledge, comfort, or entertainment. Why? Because of your time investment. This is referred to as the sunk cost. But life is too short to spend it on something that does nothing more than chew off a chunk of your clock.

Behavioral economist Dan Ariely speaks to the sunk cost fallacy in his book, *Predictably Irrational.* He writes that when factoring the costs of any exchange, we tend to focus more on what we might lose in the bargain than on what we stand to gain. The thinking being that even though the future holds more promise, we tend to heed the coattail tug of things in which we've already made an investment–monetarily or emotionally. Over the long-term this can derail us from making the best, most rational choices.

This also applies to the *people* in our lives. We spend time and energy with (or around) people that can be life vacuums, sucking the marrow right out of us. You know the ones. It's either a depressing or a confrontational interaction most every time they are around. They're like really bad tenants; luring the landlord into a false sense of hope and complacency, gain access, trash the place, disregard the property and the owner's wishes, don't pay their rent, and then disappear into the night.

You don't need those type of people hanging around. Absorb the sunk cost and move on. You'll make poor choices and decisions that, in hindsight, you might wish you hadn't. Chalk those learnings up to life experience and move on. Learn the lessons, but don't let old decisions cloud your judgment in the decisions you're making now. Learn from them, acknowledge them, then let it live in its proper home—the past.

"For the past 33 years, I have looked in the mirror every morning and asked myself: 'If today were the last day of my life, would I want to do what I am about to do today?' And whenever the answer has been 'No' for too many days in a row, I know I need to change something."

~ Steve Jobs

Am I important to you?

You're busy. Frustrated. Finding it hard to focus and difficulty concentrating. Myriad distractions. You know - a typical day.

Those tough days get more problematic when you're placed in a position of choosing between completing an important task and giving in to another's wants. Specifically, when you are frazzled, on deadline, or behind schedule, and your child, partner, or co-worker interrupts because they want your attention. (Not to mention the phone, text chimes, email notifications, and doorbells). It would be natural at that high energy moment to say something along the lines of, "this isn't a good time for me." And that's a perfectly normal response. Unfortunately human nature and ego are such that what those other people *hear* is, "I'm not important to you."

Here's some food for thought. Someone working fulltime (40 hours a week, 2080 hours a year) from age 21 (and many of us enter the job market well before then) till age 65 (and many choose to continue working past that age), will spend over 91,000 hours of their life at work. Compare that to the 2 – 3 hours a day you have left to spend with your loved ones. That's some brutal math right there (and also a compelling reason to do what you love).

Of course, we can't always drop everything without notice to accommodate all the people all the time. It's wiser (and more productive) to establish ground rules. For instance, if you work from home, you might incorporate a policy where you'd like quiet/work time from 8am–1pm. Emergencies? Fine. Just be sure to define what constitutes an emergency. Make the distinction between *wants* and *musts*. Brainstorm work-a-rounds with others that are affected. How about installing an in-box outside your work area? Or perhaps a chalkboard where others can leave notes and requests. Whatever works best for you.

The key is establishing, communicating, and then adhering to those ground rules. They may not be perfect for everyone, but it beats being constantly frazzled and frustrated and is far better than having significant people hear, "I'm not important to you."

"Most of us spend too much time on what is urgent and not enough time on what is important."

~ Stephen Covey

Are we still friends?

One of the more singular interpersonal challenges is reconciling why some friendships end. Everything is peachy keen, you get together every now and then, chat on the phone periodically, and occasionally swap random cartoon and chuckle-filled emails. Then, for no specific reason you can point to, the relationship slips away.

The fact is, people come and go throughout life. Some appearing for just a moment (the barista that gave you a friendly smile), some brief but frustrating (the police officer that gave you a speeding ticket), and some enlightening (your favorite teacher, as example). Some hang around for a day, some a month, and a few for a lifetime. Some of those we might have a bit of influence on (naturally, short of imprisonment, no one person has complete control over another), while some outcomes will be determined by others.

Through it all though, friends can—and do—come and go. Either you didn't take charge of the connections, others didn't, or it really didn't seem to matter to anyone one way or the other. Some hold the niche of being in another's life for a reason or only a season. That's okay. Akin to David Carradine in the 1970's TV series *Kung Fu*, get in, find and fulfill your purpose, then move on.

Like romantic relationships, ended friendships usually leave a trail of breadcrumbs that will piece together what happened. Before overthinking things though, consider: some friendships simply have an expiration date. They serve their purpose and life goes on. While this is frustrating, it's also a good opportunity to take a look back to determine that purpose, and to grasp and embrace the value of that connection and life lesson.

Still, why do friendships end? Perhaps you were brought together by a common denominator (a gym, book club, professional organization, child activities, work peers, etc.), then one of you moved away. No other connection, so the purpose of that friendship was fulfilled. Both of you got something from the friendship and it was time to move on.

Whatever the reason, don't beat yourself up about it. Just because something doesn't last forever doesn't lessen its impact or value. Making a difference in other's lives makes a difference in your life. If you speak only a few sentences to someone you met just that one time, your actions still carry the weight that can make a lifetime of difference. A small piece of everyone you cross paths with remains with you both.

"Consider others' interests as important as your own ... People are looking out for number one, but the way to leave a legacy is to also look out for others."

~ Jim Rohn

If you find it funny, you find it funny. That's (your) life.

Short of physically assaulting you, no one should be able to *make* you feel anything you choose not to. This is a controversial stance with plenty of people willing to take a side. Here's mine. You can *choose* to be happy or sad or hurt. Someone may say or do something that brings about certain feelings in you, but short of assault, they can't create feelings that you don't hold to be true. They can try to force their feelings on you, but you have the option of ignoring, rejecting, or accepting them. As important, you can choose how, or even if, you react to them.

Similarly, you can't force specific feelings simply because you believe you're supposed to. As example, if your aunt trips and sends a platter of marinara-soaked pasta crashing to the tiled kitchen floor, you might believe you should feel badly, while in fact you find it hilarious. Once you have ascertained that no one was injured in the redecorating effort, you'd likely laugh about it.

So, who had control of your emotions in that case? Your aunt? You? I'd venture it's as much to do with the moment, your personality, and your mood. Some you control, some you can't, but, in this instance, no other person forced feelings of empathy or humor on you. They might have tried, though. "Why are you laughing? That was not funny!" or, "Someone could have been hurt!" You get the idea.

Sometimes others aren't trying to force their feelings on you but simply don't understand *your* feelings. Sometimes people believe they are saying what they should be saying during a specific circumstance (see above). But saying what you believe you should say can be an entirely different animal than simply saying what you believe.

Not a soul can command that you share in their feelings if you are not of mind to. Remembering that is an important step in owning your life. You'll experience the entire spectrum of emotions many times over, and often not in a silo. As example, sometimes things might seem so pitiful that you've no choice but to laugh. You own your emotions. Be loving (or desirous or angry or empathetic, etc.), because it comes from within you, *not* because someone demands it of you. Trust in yourself.

"Your intellect may be confused, but your emotions will never lie

to you."

~ Roger Ebert

What did you just say?

We sometimes engage in conversation simply to hear agreement or get validation of our existing beliefs. In those instances, we're hearing, but not listening. Basically, just mentally searching for the source of a trivial, disagreeable breeze so we can slam the window of engagement shut. Give this a try instead: At the end of a conversation, meeting, or call, get into a habit of taking a moment and asking yourself, "What did I learn?"

All of our interactions are valuable in their own way. Getting the most out of them requires practicing your active listening skills. Listen to what the other person is saying and then paraphrase it back. i.e. "What I'm hearing you say is..." This lets the other person know you are listening and keeps you engaged and focused.

A significant challenge is refraining from ambushing the conversation. Ambushing occurs when you are listening to someone, practicing active listening, but only for the purpose of looking for holes or a perceived flaw; ignoring the other person's intent altogether. This is analogous with the *myside bias* which refers to the tendency to evaluate other people's statements only to reply in such a way as to prove your original beliefs. Why? Well, as Charlie Sheen might say, "WINNING!" If you remember that meltdown, then you'll recognize how fruitless the behavior can be in the long run.

~ Ask yourself: *"Am I seeking knowledge or looking for something that validates my existing belief?"* ~

Hey look everyone – I *Am* Somebody!

Greeks began staging Olympic Games and lauding the heroics of winning athletes in 776 BC. While that was an early documented way to recognize individual accomplishment, we've been craving attention and recognition for thousands of years.

Just as we love hearing our own voice or our own name, we love bragging to the world how special we are. And one way society has long used to demonstrate recognition, accomplishment, and a sense of fellowship is with diploma-size slips of paper, pint-size statuettes, and pieces of shiny medal.

These can take form as (here we go): trophies, medals, keys to a city, honorary degrees, certificates of achievement, marriage and professional licensing, grammar, middle, high school, vocational, technical school, college and university diplomas and degrees, gold or platinum records, Nobel prize, Oscars, Emmys, Grammys, FFA ribbons for best goat or cow, employee of the month (Ooh– parking space. Score!), Cub Scout patches, Girl Scout sashes, bumper stickers, decals, flags, and pennants.

We work hard (for many of these), we're proud, and we relish the attention. We display these symbols of recognition by framing, mounting, hanging, and backlighting them. We boldly and proudly thump our chest for the world. Partly to satiate our ego and partly for others to admire, respect, and hopefully compliment us on our marvelous and magnificent achievements. We hold parties, events, galas. We can't wait to post the related photos and videos. These may not be demonstrable proof of ability, but it's what we're accustomed to. Our symbols of achievement.

Some people attend day or weekend classes as much for a sense of self-worth and pride as for scholarly pursuit. Some people like to collect a swarm of letters after their name to show, enhance, or validate their expertise in a field (or at least show they did what needed to be done for the acronyms). Depending on your field of interest, you could harvest a virtual alphabet to use after your name by attending a week-long series of classes. The diplomas looks great and by Gawd, it sure does feel good. And why not? It shows that you *are somebody.* (Clue–you always were.)

Through it all, pay attention and absorb the experiences. How they enhance your life and bring you closer to your goals. Applaud yourself for seeking the opportunities, and yes, relish the attention that comes your way every now and again.

Before we move on, don't forget about the attention and recognition you give in your romantic life. Challenge yourself to show that special person *how* they are important and *why* they matter. It'd be easy if it was as simple as giving a "Dad of the Year" mug or an "I love you" certificate. You know, just like giving flowers on Valentine's Day. Easy peasey. Your work is done. Nope. Now your work begins. And, it lasts a lifetime.

"Don't worry when you are not recognized but strive to be worthy

of recognition."

~ Abraham Lincoln

The facts don't change *our* facts.

When you're arguing with someone, both you and the other person are trying to do at least one of two things: provide factual evidence that supports your position and thus share knowledge, or, attempt to establish intellectual dominance or superiority over the other person, regardless of facts. Those two things are independent of one another (often to the topic as well) and can lead to acrimonious behavior.

Let's use organized debates as example. You are assigned to Team A, and are tasked with defending an issue that you might not know much about, don't care about, and in which you have nothing at stake. You dive in, do some research, map out potential pitfalls, and create a compelling argument. Right or wrong, you're prepared to defend your position. This is where confirmation bias enters the equation.

Confirmation bias (sometimes called "myside bias") is when you only seek information that validates your argument or beliefs. This is easy to fall into because most of us are more biased towards confirming our beliefs than being open minded to information that might suggest our initial conclusions were inaccurate (read: *wrong*). I'd venture to guess that there are few people who enjoy being wrong or having it brought to their attention (humiliation), but many who are willing to argue for hours on end to support their beliefs–right or wrong. And the stronger we believe about something or the more important the topic is to us, the more entrenched the bias becomes. This leads us to dismiss information or arguments that contradict what we choose to believe as fact.

There's an easy answer, but no easy action. You can ask someone to have an open mind, you can tell yourself that you are open-minded (bet you can make all kinds of arguments to prove it, too!), but putting it into play with another of the same ilk takes patience, understanding, and a willingness for mutual resolution. Confirmation bias tramples a wide path—from the dining room table to the underpinnings of politics and foreign relations. We all want what we want and will argue or wage war to get it.

"Blessed are the hearts that can bend; they shall never be broken."

~ Albert Camus

Always being right is wrong.

If you're mired in a heated conversation with the goal of being right, then you're already wrong. Being right doesn't mean a thing, (especially) if you are the only one sticking around to hear about it. Many of us have a competitive nature and are hardwired to win, to dig our feet in and stand our ground. But in the real world, it can be counterproductive.

How strong is your need to be right and what are you willing to risk to claim the title of "Mr. Know it All"? Always having to be right is no more an indicator of intelligence than believing that yelling at someone increases their comprehension. Neither is true and in both cases you come away looking like an ass.

By steadfastly convincing yourself that it's "your way or the highway," you give away options and creative alternatives, risk personal and professional relationships, miss learning new ideas, and perhaps most important—lose the opened-minded humility accompanying the braced realization that you are not, and will never be, always right. Admitting when you are wrong can be another way of saying that you just learned something new.

Some people insist they are right simply because admitting they might be in error would be embarrassing. So they defend their position, fighting tooth and nail to gain intellectual dominance and agreement. As French author André Maurois famously wrote, "Everything that is in agreement with our personal desires seems true. Everything that is not puts us into a rage." The truth though is that none of us can be right about everything. Recognizing that, and knowing that there are many alternative, yet-to-be discovered perspectives, is nothing to be ashamed of. The world isn't flat after all. We learned, we drew new maps, and made globes. Life progressed.

One more note on this subject. We all like the sound of our own voice and to hear our name from others. You want someone to like you? Call them by name and genuinely listen to what they are saying. Talk *with* them, not to them. Want to be alienated and seen as the office (or relationship) egomaniacal blowhard? Easy. Never listen, always interrupt, and proclaim that whatever you have to say is gospel and without need to continue the conversation. There. You did it. Everyone officially loathes you, no one wants to be around you, you're never included or invited to functions, and people avoid you like the plague. But hey–damn it, you were right! Now go home and tell the cat or dog about it.

"The opinion of 10,000 people is of no value if none of them know anything about the subject."

~ Attributed to Roman Emperor Marcus Aurelius

No harm, no foul.

"What are you saying? That's not true! You're crazy–that's just B.S.!"

Sometimes it's difficult to accept others simply for who they are. Especially when they don't agree with your vision of how things ought to be.

Unfortunately, accepting someone at face value isn't always the "go to" choice. Saying that someone rubs you the wrong way is just a polite way of saying that you don't agree with them or, perhaps, the way they choose to live. Because they are, well, different. The issue there is that we are *all* different.

Part of accepting others includes accepting chunks of their personality that drive you nuts. A compulsive gossip, as example. It might be better to just accept him as a busybody and take that into consideration with future interaction. After all, if no harm is done to another and it's not illegal, they have as much right to be who they are as you do to be who you are—whether they like it or you like it or not. Seek common ground and be open just as you would want others to do for you. Maybe it works, or maybe there are too many differences to celebrate. While we all want to be ourselves; many of us are nonetheless pissed off by others exercising that same individuality.

I don't have to agree with your views on politics, sex, or religion. But I should respect those views, just as I desire the same respect for my beliefs. You cannot demand to be who you are and also demand everyone else to be who you are as well. Because let me tell you, if you're waiting for people to line up around the block just to kiss your ass and tell you they how wrong they are about things—grab a sofa and a snack. It's gonna be a long wait.

You can argue long and hard about how man never landed on the moon, or how the chicken came before the egg, or that contrails are actually chemtrails, or how Katie Perry is so much more talented than Miley Cyrus, or ... well, you get the idea.

It's not always better having to be right. Sometimes it's better to just be.

"I would rather have a mind opened by wonder than one closed by belief."

~ Gerry Spence

Sit. Roll-over. Shake my hand.

Going into a relationship thinking you can change the other person is a recipe for disaster. Primarily, because most of us don't want to be told what to do, when to do it, nor how to do it. As important, that other person has their own devious little plot to do the same to you. It reminds me of the saying about how women marry men hoping they'll change and men marry women hoping they won't.

Dogs represent great examples of instilling behavior without changing the core being. You can train your dog, but you can't change it. You can dress it in silly clothes, put shoes on it, or paint its nails. But it will always be a dog. If barking bothers you, you shouldn't get a dog that can bark—because it's going to bark. Who would you expect would change—the dog or you? A dog can be trained, but it's still going to live its life as a dog. And most dogs bark. (You knew that before you got the dog, right?)

Maybe dogs are onto something. One of the secrets to a joyful life is seeing things and people as fresh and new, always anticipating the next walk, car ride, or journey, and eagerly anticipating a little treat now and again.

And funny thing, I was just chatting with your dog and he told me he's going to train you to chase squirrels. I told him it'll never happen, but he says he can change you. Weird, huh?

"The depressing thing about tennis is that no matter how good I get, I'll never be as good as a wall."

~ Mitch Hedberg

Feeling a little drained?

I was talking with a friend about how some people habitually use others for their own benefit, regardless of the detrimental impact on the person being used. My friend, a very creative sort, refers to them as *energy stalkers*. I asked her how she came up with that and she said, "They come across as friends but then they change before our eyes. Their smile disappears along with whatever it was that they wanted from you." They arrive, under the guise of friendship, only to reap for their own benefit and then you don't see them again until they want something.

Energy stalkers can be anywhere. From those people who think they know more about what you want or need than you do (and can't wait to straighten you out!), to those who espy a naive or overly-trusting person and lure them into use. This can take place in both personal and business relationships (energy stalkers are equal opportunity users). Anyone and any place where a person can be used for the benefit of another, they'll be floating around, waiting.

Energy stalkers are opportunistic bone pickers, taking what they can use—money, physical attributes, and energy—draining their victims for personal gain, and then disappearing. Until next time. They'll tell you it's all for you. But in reality, for them you are just a tool. A soul to reap, harvest, and discard. In lay terms—users.

"If you give someone permission to do something, you also give up

your right to complain about it if they take you up on it."

~ Michael

131

Copycat, copycat!

No matter the race you're running, you are only running it against yourself. Running other people's races or chasing other people's dreams is pointless. You can't win their race for them and you're the only one that can complete yours.

Running other people's races also means chasing their perceived successes (read: celebrity). We dress like him, talk like her, live like them. Where do you fit into your life? This extends beyond imitating our famous brethren. The keep-up-with-the-Joneses syndrome is alive and well. Weigh 115 and you'll want to weigh 112. 5'11"? Why can't you be 6'2"? Brunette? Maybe you should try blonde. Blonde? Try Red. Red? Damn freckles! Round and round we go. That's why there'll always be fashion shows, auto shows, bridal shows, footwear shows, and shows devoted to helping you produce shows. I wonder what would happen if we all woke up one day and said, "Hum. I'm good just as I am."

What are we trying to accomplish by imitating someone? I once posed that question to a group and someone replied that it was "a hobby." A hobby fueled by a throng of celebrity-centered publications, web sites, blogs, television shows, and so on. We simply cannot get enough of other peoples' lives. If we spent as much time learning and burrowing into our own lives as we do wondering what celebrity X is wearing, or where a favorite musician eats dinner, we'd have people following *us* around!

Let's bring it full circle to the train wreck. The much anticipated (yes, you do) celebrity meltdown. Brittany Spears, Lindsay Lohan, Charlie Sheen, et al. What's the fascination? Well, we finally get the chance to poke an imaginary finger at them and say, "Aha!, you are a person same as me!" (They always were.) Do you gain enjoyment from another person's misery because you feel they have it coming because of an arrogant, pompous attitude, or is it a simple jealousy of their perceived lifestyle (of which you really know nothing about)? It might be escapism from your reality, but it is very much a life-reality for them.

What's at the core of celebrity fixation? Why do we believe them to be so much different or better than "common folk?" Perhaps it's because they *appear* to be living the lives that many of us wish we were living. They have accomplished something or achieved a goal to become a celebrity. They have fame, power, and money. And, unfortunately, seemingly as often, they are famous just for being famous. Wealth and arrogance can do that for you.

See what we're circling? They get *attention*. And who are they getting it from? Those who would be better served living their own lives. Good news! There's a choice. You can lay the red carpet and hang the lights or you can walk the red carpet under the lights. If you chose to be a bystander, it's just that—your choice. No bitching and moaning about others, and no pity parties. Want to see someone on a pedestal? Put yourself on one. That's not ego. That's common sense.

"Don't be so obsessed with becoming so thoroughly awesome and amazing that you forget you already are."

~ Michael

Careful! Most cats have claws.

My other half likes cats. My other half *loves* cats. Correspondingly, my other half adores her two cats. Now, cats devour a stinky, nasty-looking, canned meat sludge that CLIO award-winning advertising gurus hawk as "*gourmet* cat food."

Her kitties have free roam of both the house and the surrounding neighborhood. They come and go as *they* please. After all, they know who the real boss is, otherwise they'd be bathing, feeding, and petting us and paying for the privilege to do so, right? But I digress.

One morning one of the cats went AWOL and didn't muster for her normal face time with the adorably decorated food dish. My other half lovingly placed the plated *gourmet* delicacy into a plastic baggie and slid it into the fridge where it would remain, waiting for cat number two to bless us with a cameo. Now, to me, placing even well-sealed cat fuel on a refrigerator shelf is akin to tossing horse meat next to my veggies.

By shopping with my other half, I know that canned cat food (at time of this occurrence) cost forty-six cents. When I discovered the cat rations in the refrigerator, I asked my other half if she'd be upset if I were to lose twenty-three cents. She looked at me like I was nuts and said "No. What a silly question." I replied, "Great!" and promptly removed the (*gourmet*) cat food from the fridge and washed it down the disposal. Well, my other half looked at me and asked, "What the @#!* are you doing?" I said, "Losing twenty-three cents."

Lesson: When you are looking to get your way; carefully consider your position, phrase your desires in a positive manner, and most important, choose your battles wisely. Seek compromise and middle ground. Oh, and don't forget to consider the other person in the equation. Cat owners can be very defensive and I'm still paying for that twenty-three cent conversation. Just saying.

"*No matter how much cats fight, there always seem to be plenty of kittens.*"

~ Abraham Lincoln

We're not in Kansas anymore.

Ever been someplace where everyone seems just a bit different than you? Or someplace where you didn't know a soul and you felt out of place? Those are learning times.

Here's a great example of a learning opportunity: The next time when you're taking a stroll or a ride, take a turn on a random street or path. A turn you wouldn't typically take. Something random that takes you out of your routine. Why? Well, because you can, but as important, because you should. Your discoveries will serve to broaden and brighten your personal horizon. You'll be surprised what you'll find just minutes from your everyday life.

"Don't be afraid." Those were reportedly Nobel laureate poet Seamus Heaney's last words. A text message (go figure) to his wife, Marie, sent while in his hospital bed. As some point or another we are all afraid of the sheer size of what's possible in life. As the old saying goes, "if it was easy, everyone would be doing it."

Here are a few more ways to put yourself in discovery mode: No kids? Visit a mall and you'll get an ice water shower wake-up call. Or, take a stroll through an exotic ethnic market. Vegan? Go to a steakhouse, order a salad, and relish the environment. Why? Discovery. You'll realize just how unique all of us are and, whether we agree on everything or not, we're all in it together.

Ever been on a road trip and missed the sign for your exit or taken a wrong turn in a strange city? What happened? You probably experienced frustration, momentary confusion, and checked your watch a time or two. Hopefully, you also took a deep breath and soaked up the experience of (involuntarily) exploring a new area. For many, an accidental nudge is the only way they step out of their comfort zone.

You won't find life's most amazing experiences on your usual path. Sometimes you need to get lost to find your way. Sometimes, you need to leave the map at home. If you don't continually evolve and progress, you'll be a one hit wonder. You probably have an all-time favorite song, but you don't want hear it all the time. That's why radio stations work off a playlist. They know you want to hear the popular stuff and the way they continue to keep it fresh and interesting is by salting in new songs along the way. You might have a favorite musical artist, painter, sculptor, or actor, but you still keep your eyes and ears open for new experiences. There's discovery in diversity.

"*Be unpredictable. Shred at an angle.*"

~ Michael

Kids are fearless!

How would it feel to be a kid again? You know, back when everything was possible. What would you do if you could do what everyone told you that you couldn't? (Say that three times fast) What challenges would you conquer? What obstacles would you hurdle? What great puzzles would you solve? Consider ...

- Henry Ford didn't have a driver license.
- Benjamin Franklin lived in a house without electricity.
- Susan B. Anthony was never allowed to vote.
- Neither Steve Jobs nor Bill Gates finished college.
- Alexander Graham Bell's wife (Mabel Gardiner Hubbard) was deaf from age 5.
- Steven Hawking - a brilliant English theoretical physicist, cosmologist, and author, remains mentally unencumbered by amyotrophic lateral sclerosis (ALS, commonly known as Lou Gehrig's Disease) since his diagnosis at age 21.
- Ludwig van Beethoven began losing his hearing at age 26 but continued composing till his death at age 56 (his infamous Symphony No. 5, was written between ages 34–38).

You get the idea. Along with many others, they all walk(ed) to the beat of their own drummer, overcame hurdles, and refused to be defeated by life's inevitable setbacks.

The route wasn't always easy or obvious. It takes determination to not accept mediocrity as life's norm. Unfortunately, many of us meander like water, following a path of least resistance. We like the concept of taking the road less traveled (Robert Frost) or the road never taken, but real life and fear of uncertainty gets in the way. Your challenge? Deny people the satisfaction of telling you something can't be done by doing it. Show the world that you can and that you will. *Make the effort.*

Here's something to chew on: if you don't do what's in your heart, you make it amazingly easy for others to believe that you can't. If you don't try, people will assume that you can't, won't, or couldn't. For instance, if you want to be known as the person who parasailed across the Grand Canyon—you at least have to make the attempt. Better to fail than play the "what if" game. And if you don't get your desired outcome? People will have a hard time disagreeing with someone who takes action; win, lose, or draw. It's been said that everything that can be done has already been. Do you believe that? (The correct answer is "no.")

You are fighting for yourself. So, what holds you back? What are you leaning on as a crutch or using as your excuse?

"*Sometimes you find yourself in the middle of nowhere, and sometimes in the middle of nowhere, you find yourself.*"

~ Unknown

Let's head to the kitchen.

Do you have a unique, one-of-a-kind, earth shaking idea? Then by all means, act *before* you do an online search and discover it's not as singular as you imagine it to be.

Snow tires are best in snow, umbrellas work for rain (but not wind), and coats provide warmth from the cold. Tons of readily available, patented, viable solutions meeting everyday life needs. Does that keep you from creating *your* unique solutions?

Let's use some basic spices, condiments, veggies, and fruits as an example. These simple ingredients are used millions of times every day to create one of a kind dishes. (In fact, Oscar Tschirky created one of the world's most recognizable salads out of those ordinary ingredients.)

To the crux of the matter: It's what you create with the ordinary–your personal recipe–that gives it your personal signature. The ingredients may be commonplace but the creation will be uniquely yours.

Oh, and before we move on, Mr. Tschirky was quite well-known as the maître d'hôtel at the Waldorf Hotel in Manhattan, NY.

"I can't because." *Three little words. Two are excuses. One incredibly powerful. Use all three prudently.*

~ Michael

Sometimes success is found through failure.

There's a saying around what you would attempt if you knew you couldn't fail. It does get one thinking, and it begs this question: What would you attempt if you knew you *would* fail? Would you still try? Would you consider it a challenge? A learning experience? Would it depend on the perceived consequences? Would you beg-off because of a deep-seated fear of failure?

There's much to be learned in failure. And since it's likely you'll fail more than you succeed, you should heed the lessons. Be able to look yourself in the mirror and know you put in the time, possessed the resolve and determination to venture a task, overcome a fear, and risk rejection or failure. There is admirable accomplishment in effort.

When you want to be the best at something, how you practice is as important as how long you practice. It isn't only about the time you put in. To achieve those seemingly quantum leaps in ability you have to mentally stretch yourself. A willingness to fail is an integral part of achieving success. Acknowledge the failure, and learn from the experience.

Knowing that you have no option but to fail at a task presents a delicious opportunity to tinker, poke, push, and squeeze. Shake it till the coins fall out! In so doing, you challenge the notion of failure, thus creating a larger vision with a deeper appreciation of success.

"Experience is merely the name men gave to their mistakes."

~ Oscar Wilde (*The Picture of Dorian Gray*)

Speaking of success.

At one time or another, we've all experienced the pangs associated with the fear of failure. Journals are bulging at their bindings of ways to overcome, to persevere, and how so and so tried 1,001 times before they saved the world. But what about the fear of *success*? The compressing fear that you might actually achieve something? That you might just ... succeed? I've met many people whose fear of succeeding far outweighed their fear of failing.

Let's define, at least in simple dictionary terms, failure and success. In this context, "failure" is *an act or instance of failing or proving unsuccessful; lack of success.* Success being *the favorable or prosperous termination of attempts or endeavors; the accomplishment of one's goals.* (Dictionary.com)

Why would anyone fear success? Being discovered a fraud? Not believing they deserve it? Low self-esteem? Insecurity? Fear of not being accepted for who they are? Afraid of scorn or ridicule? Rejection? The excuses are endless. What if simply by *being*, you are successful? Take, as example, a painting you don't understand, feel a monkey could have created, yet others are throwing hundreds of thousands or millions of dollars at the artist. Certainly she was able to overcome any internal fears of failure, rejection, or success. What you think didn't matter to the artist. The artist did as she pleased anyway and let the chips fall where they will.

Many find it easier to pledge devotion and allegiance to a sports team or a favorite brand than they do to themselves. Proudly wearing shirts, caps, and jackets emblazed with a favorite team or brand, but when it comes to the #1 product and brand in life (hint: check the mirror), it's nowhere to be found.

Labels are only meaningful to the person that creates them. It's a perception based ideology. If someone tries to jump a gully four times and lands in the creek each time, some will call him a loser. Someone else may find him fatuous or think him stupid. Another might tag him as persistent or determined. All are based on individual perception. The thing is, you can't live your life based on other's perceptions and perspectives. The only label that you should care about is the one you sew into your psyche. That's the one you'll live with.

Like risking failure, success means leaving your comfort zone. That diminutive room without windows. Climb out. Redefine what constitutes success. Frankly, you are a success simply by being, so you may as well show the world who that person is and let the chips fall where they may. No one will be looking at you as critically or as harshly as you're looking at yourself, and at the end of the day it's your opinion of you that matters. You are not branded with anyone else's label. Let others paint their painting. You create your own masterpiece. You'll find that it's impossible to fail at that.

"Existence is a series of footnotes to a vast, obscure, unfinished

masterpiece."

~ Vladimir Nabokov

You have sight, but how about vision?

Ask yourself, "What would you do if you were not afraid?" It's most often not about getting a chance, but *taking* a chance. If you don't go after what you want, you'll never have it. If you don't ask, the answer is always no. If you don't move forward, you're always in the same place.

It boils down to this: If you always do what you've always done you'll never know what you can become. This is a spin of the old "if you always do what you've always done, you'll always get what you always got." By the way, that is simply not true. Twenty-five years ago, few of us used email. Back in the 1980s, facsimile machines were an exciting, cutting edge technology. While FAX technology isn't yet obsolescent, I'll bet you use it less often than in years past. It's unique and rare all over again. (A polite way of saying "old.")

The point: doing what you've always done with an expectation of getting what you've always gotten is no longer realistic. If you do what you've always done and you'll get left behind by people willing to adapt and embrace change in the world and in their lives. Nostalgia = good. Head in the sand = bad. A wonderful thing about the past is that you can revisit it, learn from it, and relive fond memories. Remember though, that learning from the past requires *understanding* the past, just as part of changing *with* the times is changing and challenging the surroundings *of* your times.

You can want something, you can wish for it, or you can go and get it. Visionaries forge new paths and part of being visionary is taking control of your life and grabbing the bull by the horns. There is no pause button. Life continues whether you choose to participate or not. You can embrace it or simply let opportunities breeze past, taking their tantalizing scent along with them. Time is the great equalizer. You have the same amount as everyone else as well as the knowledge of knowing the clock and calendar are very predictable.

Don't confuse vision with focus. Your vision represents your goals and aspirations. Your focus is the plan and path you forge to achieve your goals. Sometimes, not seeing things clearly is a blessing in disguise. It challenges you to continually refine your focus. To keep going when things are not ceremoniously presented to you on a silver platter. An opportunity to think and strategize until whatever it is becomes clear. Sometimes it requires patience or a little meditation. Sometimes you have to be more proactive and remove the haze on your own. The sun's always out somewhere, even if you can't readily see it.

Here's a personal example: I was having a CT scan due to a recent injury. I was told to remain perfectly still for the duration of the procedure (34 minutes). I realized just how many body parts can simultaneously itch when you can't scratch them (the answer is *all* of them). I also discovered that when you can't move your body that your mind will fill the void. I kept coming up with ideas (that I couldn't make note of) and found myself inventing rhymes so that I would remember to scribble them down once unfettered. What started as a serious dent in my day's schedule became very relaxing and productive. In fact, you're reading about it now.

Inspiration can come at any time and from any place. Even run-of-the-mill everyday stuff. Perhaps something on TV (including commercials) or a song lyric. Where do you feel and experience your creative spirit? Maybe a pottery or a glass-blowing class, meditation, perhaps a long, invigorating walk? What rouses and stokes your personal flame and keeps you going? A spike of creativity and sense of accomplishment (often accompanied by a heightened sense of self-worth) is an amazing high. What's yours? How do you grasp it, keep it, grow and shape it? How do you open yourself to it?

I frequently generate ideas late in the evening or early morning hours so I keep a digital recorder next to my bed. During those quiet times, my mind is uncluttered from the day's realities. I've solved the world's ills many times over in my sleep. Before using the recorder, I'd swear that I'd remember my thoughts when I woke and jot them down then. No such luck. I'd remember having a vivid flash of self-proclaimed brilliance but nary a clue as to what it was all about. Anyway, I suppose that one of my Aha! moments was simply to use the recorder to record my Aha! moments. Not Einstein level thinking, but it works for me.

"Sometimes the boomerang comes back into your hand, sometimes into the back of your head. Depends on if and where you're looking for it."

~ Michael

Peek-A-Boo.

More than ten percent of the U.S. population fesses up to suffering from nyctophobia (or achluophobia)—more commonly known as being afraid of the dark. Yet those same 30+ million people will wander around dangerous places in broad daylight. Why? Believing that there's no surprises lurking in shadows? That apparitions or zombies only come out at night? That the hand only reaches out from under the bed after midnight?

Maybe it's simply because with light, things are easily seen and appear tangible and concrete? Without surprise? Perhaps. Try this: Look around and pick up something within reach. An object. Any object. Now turn off the light. It's still there; unchanged. You're just experiencing it from a different perspective. You have the benefit and comfort of *knowing* what it is and because you picked it up and were holding it *before* the lights went out (like that teddy bear you clutch when the floor creaks in the middle of the night).

Consider the summer months of July and August. They look much different to a nine-year-old than to a working adult. To a child, those two months hold a year of life. For most adults, the days go by as usual. For school age children though, the possibilities of summer are endless. It comes down to expectations and perspective. Two things you control. And by paying close attention to them both, you can also change and control your *perception* of things—including whatever you chose to believe is hiding in the closet of that unlit, creaky-floored room.

The truth is, *everything* is an unknown at one time or another. And everything remains an unknown until you choose to use your internal light source (i.e. your senses, *including* common sense). You can trip and fall just as easily on a sidewalk at noon as in a cobweb-laden attic at midnight.

The key word in the phrase, "fear of the dark," is fear. You cannot allow yourself to be held captive by fear. To be controlled by the gut-wrenching, sweaty palm "what ifs." This holds true even more so for your life goals. Your dreams. They can't be kept locked away in a box filled with fear (i.e. "I can't," "it would never work"). Set them free. Once they are clear in your mind's eye, they're no longer hiding in the dark. They're within grasp. In light: *plain as day.* It may represent change, but most worthwhile things do. You can't learn to swim on the sidewalk. Go. Do. Night or day. It's not a leap of faith. It's having faith in your leap.

"No matter how fast light travels it finds [that] the darkness has always got there first, and is waiting for it."
~ Sci-Fi Author Terry Pratchett

Race the sunrise!

"It's going to be one of those days." Guess what. They're *all* going to be one of those days. That's life. The world really doesn't care that you are having a lousy day. (That too, is crappy, isn't it?) Get used to it, get over it, and get on with making the best of each and every one you have remaining. Attitude doesn't overcome everything, but feeling like the entire world is against you isn't going to solve anything either.

Not to sound like every motivational poster in every gym or Pinterest page you've ever visited, but, you really *must* believe in yourself. You can have bad days; we all do. But self-belief will see you through those times when you feel that everything you do is a bust. Believing in yourself (even when others don't seem to) gives you an inner-edge. You'll find your thought process slowly changing. Over time you'll discover that what once seemed impossible becomes more and more "what if" and less "I can't."

There is no better time than right now—today—to get with it. How long can you afford to wait? Now is your best chance to live a fully consuming life. Make *now* a precious time because this now will never come again. The clock isn't slowing down for any of us.

Part of living fully is facing the things that keep you up at night. (Your awaiting adventures!) You should neither run nor hide from them. Get out of the shadows; embrace every twist, each sudden blind curve, and every bend. Live not as a spectator but as a thirsty observer and active participant in your own life. Trying to avoid life's random pain and inevitable fears is like living with an excruciating toothache for weeks or months simply to avoid a sixty minute dental appointment. Sack up and face your fears. Your greatest achievements and your proudest memories will come from those times. Everyone does the easy stuff.

Of course, this means you'll have to dig deep inside yourself to where the spooky stuff lives. And when you're there rooting around, if you don't find anything that scares the bejesus out of you–keep digging. It's in there. Close your eyes if you must, but keep your mind open. Stop putting things off and waiting for a better opportunity. The one thing none of us can control is the clock. It's the great equalizer. Steve Jobs, Shakespeare, Picasso, da Vinci, Einstein, Babe Ruth (well, you get the idea) had the exact same amount of time in any given day as you. Make *now* your time. Make *today* your day.

"Every strike brings me closer to the next home run."

~ Babe Ruth

Limits. You set them, you can beat them.

"I don't think I can do that." Sound familiar? Try. The alternative is to continue to doubt your abilities, and eventually paint yourself into a corner where you feel completely inept. If you really want to doubt something, doubt your limits. Here's an easy way to start on this path.

First, ask yourself why you set limits that mentally keep you from new experiences. Then, remove those barriers one at a time, gradually extending your limits. Try this: When someone asks you to do something out of your comfort zone, mentally assign it a number on a scale of 1–7, where 1 is, "no-problemo," and 7 is, "Nope. Not going to happen." Then consider what it would take to gradually get you from a terrifying situation (7) to something you can reasonably tackle (2 or 3).

Address your fears (yes, those little gremlins are constantly lurking) one at a time. Break it down into steps as you would a large chore, until you can plausibly see yourself completing the task. Set a *reachable* time limit for each progressive step.

Let's use skydiving as an example. Don't tell yourself that skydiving terrifies you. Instead, try, "one day I will go skydiving." Now begin making it concrete. This week you consider how great it will feel to accomplish this feat. You envision the certificate proudly displayed on your wall. You envision telling your friends about it. Proud? Great! You've moved down from a petrifying 7 to a 6. Next week, you visit a jump center and talk with an instructor. She shows you everything involved, the safety features, and shares her experiences. You talk with other neophytes who also share your fears. You begin thinking, "I can do this!" Now you're at a 4 of

7. You're still afraid, but you're addressing your concerns a step at a time, coming closer to facing the fear.

Finally, the big day comes. You steel your nerves, climb into the plane, scared to tears but now envisioning the fulfilling result. The tales you'll tell! You overcame the fear—even if for only a short while. Two hours later, you're framing the jump certificate and bragging about it to everyone within earshot. You're rightfully proud. You're still terrified, but you know that the pride and accomplishment will stay with you throughout life. Congratulations are in order.

"There's a palpable tension between what we strive to achieve and the fight with memories of past attempts."

~ Michael

Try the window!

There are always *at least* two sides to every story. An episode of the long running CBS sitcom, *The Big Bang Theory*, offers a great analogy. Amy (played by Mayim Bialik), a neuroscientist and character Sheldon Cooper's love interest, tries to help the obsessive-compulsive Sheldon (Jim Parsons), with his closure obsession. (Sheldon lives in a world where the word "desultory" does not exist.) They play a game of tic-tac-toe using a whiteboard and dry erase markers. As the game progresses, it reaches the stage where Sheldon announces that the conclusion is obvious; it must either result in a tie or a win for him. At this point, Amy grabs an eraser and clears the whiteboard before a stunned Sheldon is able to take his turn and claim victory.

In another example, Amy also tries to help Sheldon by leading him through a series of exercises. In one, she tells him that they live in a world where closure is not always an op ... Sheldon waits as Amy plays with her fingernails and otherwise chooses not to complete the word, before Sheldon, who can't take it any longer, shouts "Shun! It's Op-shun!"

Lesson? We don't always get the closure we desire nor the results we feel we deserve. Sometimes it's neither heads nor tails, win nor lose. But that doesn't mean you shouldn't keep moving and steering towards your life goals and desires. You might not get what you want when you want it, but it beats waiting for that "perfect moment" (I know, I know ... you'll do it tomorrow. Or when it's sunny. Or when your back doesn't hurt. Or after you ...).

This reminds me of a saying that goes something like this: "No matter how many mistakes you make or how slow you progress, you are still way ahead of someone who isn't trying." While it is true you will never accomplish your goals if you don't begin down the path, it's also healthy to be able to recognize when it's time to move on to other projects. Giving up isn't a sign of physical or mental weakness. (It's an "op-shun!") Sometimes it means you are strong enough and smart enough to let go and try a different approach. If you can't get the door to open, try the window!

While it is desirous to continue striving and reaching and seeking, it is also noble and humbling to learn the art of leaving things undone. That in itself is a form of closure. And also of continued effort, using a different tacking strategy. That's not contradictory. It's complementary.

"Some people believe holding on and hanging in there are signs of great strength. However, there are times when it takes much more strength to know when to let go and then do it."
~ Esther "Eppie" Lederer (Ann Landers)

Are you just going to sit there till you can't get up?

Patience is virtuous ... Good things come to those who wait ...

While I agree with the principles, I can't agree that following those axioms will prove beneficial in all situations. Patience isn't always a virtue. Sometimes patience is just a leaning post; an excuse for inaction. It's easier to say you're being patient than it is to get off your rear and create action. Sure, some things require patience—bird watching comes to mind. That's an activity in which John James Audubon could create a lively and valid argument about the necessity of patience.

While you're waiting, remember that other axiom about patience: A watched pot never boils. *Especially* if you don't turn on the burner. We sit around, mentally twiddling our thumbs, waiting for something magical to happen, while doing nothing to give it a push. We wait for the water to boil, but never start the fire.

You have to find what ignites your internal fire. You can't expect fairies to swoop in and toss a handful of pixie dust at you. There's no magic involved—if you don't know what you want to do, do a little of a lot. Few are blessed with a calling at a young age. We learn passion, drive, and desire through life experience. You won't know if something stirs in you until you give it a try.

Always be patient and there's but one guarantee: Death. And don't fool yourself—the end of the world comes to thousands of people each and every day. Patience is a death sentence, and on your death bed, you'll regret what you haven't done the most. You know—those things you were *patiently* waiting for just the right time to do.

Okay. So you want to see your plants in bloom and enjoy the sunset. But there's an entire day to live before the sun gives way to the horizon. Go out—explore. Do. Be. You'll find it. Maybe not today. Maybe not tomorrow, but you will. And while you're looking? Yup. That's that thing called *life*.

" The two most important days in your life are the day you are born and the day you find out why."

~ Mark Twain

Take a hike!

Most of us living in developed countries thrive in domesticated environments. Domestication, by definition, is losing the ability or desire to live or exist in the wild. This poses a question: Were we born to be (and destined to remain) domesticated?

Sure, we sow our wild oats and let our hair down every now and again, but it's still part of a domesticated life. Our truly wild, untamed side has long since faded. (Not having TV, phone, or streaming video is not considered living wild. Primitive to some, but not wild.)

Where's the tipping point between evolution and domestication? What do we lose or give up as part of becoming domesticated? What skills or abilities of ourselves (besides physical) become dull or numb by walking out of the wilderness and into a living room?

Mick Dodge* uses this analogy as part of what being closer to nature–to the wild– teaches us:

> Follow your bare soles. The first thing that happens when you step out of shoes, or the shoe box is you have to 'pay attention.' Then comes 'acceptance' learning to accept the habitat and the habits that you have. These two steps, attention and acceptance form into a stride of awareness, and the first thing that you need to be aware of is shoe salesmen and you are your own best shoe salesman.

If you think about it, life itself is a trek in the wilderness. Unpredictable, with surprises and twists lurking around every corner and along the paths we follow or forge. One of the joys of shedding a bit of urban domestication every now and then is the incredible feeling of intertwining with nature; stepping away from the metropolitan herd and creating time to discover your unique path through life. The path only you can walk. So, go on. Take a hike!

* Mick Dodge, the "barefoot sensei" from The Legend of Mick Dodge, *a reality-based show that aired in the United States on National Geographic television.*

"I'll be different, but somewhere lost inside me there'll always be the person I am tonight."
~ F. Scott Fitzgerald

One step at a time.

The United States Secret Service was created on July 5, 1865 in Washington, D.C., tasked with stopping an overwhelming counterfeit currency problem facing the US. The legislation creating the agency was on Abraham Lincoln's desk April 14, 1865, the night he was assassinated by John Wilkes Booth at Ford's Theatre in Washington D.C.

Even so, the ironic timing was probably but a footnote, as it took another 36 years and the 1901 assassination of President William McKinley in Buffalo, New York for Congress to informally request the Secret Service to provide presidential protection. And it wasn't until 1902 that full-time responsibility for presidential protection formally became Secret Service responsibility.

The United States Government was slow to recognize the change that needed to occur if it was to prevent such events in the future. Unfortunately, it took senseless tragedy to prompt the citizenry's elected representatives to take action and address complications of national, international, and human significance. Because of politics, internal bickering, power struggles, and no relatable provenance, something of paramount need, something with life and death consequences, was years in the making (sound familiar?).

You face similar hurdles and challenges in your personal life. You'll come to multiple crossroads where you'll have to choose to do nothing or to be proactive, face your fears, and strive for the life that you might otherwise avoid. You mustn't sit and wait for some mysterious tragedy (however you define it) to occur before making positive life changes. Every day you do nothing, you are one day closer to dying.

If you want something to change in your life, you have to change personally. You can't expect to become what you want by staying what you are. So—what are your excuses for delaying change? What will it take for you to commit to personal change? And what small step will you take today?

"You are the way you are because that's the way you want to be. If you really wanted to be any different, you would be in the process of changing right now."

~ Fred Smith, Founder of Federal Express

Luck? Don't (always) count on it.

Leaving life to whimsy, chance, or kismet seems romantic; like something right out of a fairy tale. And there is something to be said for whimsy and chance. It keeps dreams and hopes alive, helping us remain open to adventure.

Of course, luck certainly seems a lot simpler if you don't look at what went into creating it. The grass always appears greener on the other side of the fence (if you're not the one maintaining it). It's like Dorothy and her gang hitting the yellow brick road for the Emerald City, in search of Oscar Zoroaster Phadrig Isaac Norman Henkle Emmannuel Ambroise Diggs, or as movie lovers everywhere refer to him, the Great and Powerful Oz. The gang were hoping he would provide what they believed they were individually lacking (but possessed all along). When they reached the Emerald City, they quickly discovered that Oz had its secrets and challenges, too.

When you see someone you believe much luckier than you, just remember, every Oz has its curtain. And once you peek behind the magic curtain, you can't unpeek. You'll learn that life isn't always easy. That there's work involved. That it isn't a coin toss—no matter how bad your day, month, or life seems to be. Grab hold. When you find nothing that seems to be going right—nothing to believe in—then start simply by believing in yourself. Amazing things *will* happen. Just as you planned? Maybe. But probably not. That's the whimsical side.

" The more you believe, the luckier you get."

I see your point, but you're wrong.

It's the little things that count. And in this case, I'm referring to a little three letter word.

This magical word is easy to spell, easy to use, and easy to understand. It can even open windows into a person's inner-most thoughts. Seriously. Want to know what someone is really thinking? I learned this little trick some years ago and I'm amazed at the high percentage of accuracy it holds. Friends, co-workers, significant other, loved ones … beware. We're listening. Here comes that little secret word.

When someone is speaking (let's use a fictional politician for this example), wait for the key word to spill from their lips. Often as not, that word is "but." Example: "We must lower the unemployment rate. We must reduce taxes. We must create new jobs. We must build more parks. *But* …" (now is when your spidey senses should be on alert), "… we cannot do these things without finding the necessary funds, getting both sides of the aisle together, and continuing to develop ways to achieve these goals." In other words, "blah, blah, blah … *but* … cannot … necessary funds … get together … develop ways …" Yep. The magic word– "but."

Remember this the next time your partner says something along the lines of, "You know I'm looking forward to spending the weekend with your family. And the 500 mile drive to get there? Bring it on! Road trip! *But* … (cover your ears - spidey siren imminent) … I just told (insert name here) that I would (insert activity here). I'm sorry, I need a rain check." Guess who's not going (and probably doesn't want to) on this little adventure?

Since "but" is such a magical, telling word, it should be used sparingly (if at all) during arguments. "But" tends to negate previous statements and nulls any apology you might be attempting to make. Consider these examples:

- I'm sorry, but ...
- I see your point, but ...
- You're right, but ...

You can see how the word "but" sucks the sincerity right out of the statements. The majority of people tend to ignore what is said before the qualifier ("but") and focus on what is said afterwards. Remove the word "but" from the above statements and you'll quickly see the difference. If your statements are sincere and congruent with your feelings, you'll not often need to use that little piece of three letter magic.

" *To know what people really think, pay attention to what they do, rather than what they say."*
~ René Descartes

What are you waiting for?

I received the following email from someone who had read an article I'd written:

> *(That) made me have some weird flash I can't explain. Why/how do you seem to know things to be so right so perfect so exact ... I have no doubt I am right in my thinking but yet totally f**ked up in my day to day living. I see, no, believe and have no doubt in my mind that what you wrote is absolute truth ... but I live so far from it it's frightening!!*

I replied:

> *Many know their chosen path but sit on the sidelines watching, only to get angry and frustrated with themselves, then get up the next day and do it all over again. Is it a fear of rejection or, as important, a fear of success, fear of the unknown, or just plain laziness (escape)?*

The point I was making to the writer was this: "What if life had no timeouts and no sidelines?" Or to put it another way (that we've all probably heard or been told in some fashion or another), "Sh*t or get off the pot!"

I recently met up with the friend that sent that email to me. At first, she was ready to continue where her correspondence left off. Namely the "I can't, I should" checklist. She saw the look on my face and abruptly changed into what was obviously a well-rehearsed spiel, suddenly professing to be happy and to having everything she wanted—a great job, a roof over her head, nice clothes, a 401K, the whole nine yards—yet it was obvious she was removed from it all. I asked what was really going on, what was gnawing at her and she replied, "I honestly don't know. I mean, I should be elated, but ..." Her voice trailed off and she gave a weak flip of her left wrist and just sat silent.

Many of us find it easy to blurt out the standard "everything is great, living the dream, I have it all," because it's easier than looking at the reality. But when there's an inner conflict, there's usually a giveaway. The voice. A look. A gesture. A sigh. Something that is saying there is unfinished business. Something missing. Something dangling *out there*. Sometimes we have everything we want except what we want most. It's your job—your personal duty—to make discovering what you want *most* Priority One of your adventure.

Too often we defer those discoveries, sometimes we delay doing even simple things that bring us contentment or comfort, and often for illogical reasons. Here's a lesson in deferred contentment I recently learned firsthand:

My other half and I had just finished taking a riverside walk on a cool, crisp morning. When we returned to the parking lot, I climbed into the passenger side of the car and buckled up. As we were leaving, I commented that I'd forgotten to take off my coat. My other half said, "So?" I replied that if I left my coat on in the car that I'd freeze when I got home. She said, "So you'd rather freeze now to avoid a possibility of being cold at home? Why not be comfortable now and put on a sweatshirt when you get home? You can do both." Touché. I was willing to defer comfort and contentment for the hope of being comfortable, *later*, when I got home.

Sometimes we have to defer things we want now to achieve a long-term goal. (I may want a huge house, but if I don't plan for it now, it isn't going to happen in the future.) The coat adventure wasn't one of those instances. Sometimes you can have it both ways. For some, it's second nature to assume that if it's good there's a catch involved. But often it's as simple as accepting the present and expecting a bright future. Put on the coat.

And, interestingly, I am content now, without a ginormous house. We've made our present house a unique, cozy *home*. Contentment and comfort come from where you look for it and your willingness to accept it.

"What keeps you from being what you want to be? If the 'what' is a 'who', check the mirror."

~ Michael

Rise and shine!

Twenty-four hours in a day. No secret there—everyone knows it and it holds true for all of us. Stephen Hawking and you. Your favorite actor and you. Favorite writer, athlete, chef, artist ... you get the idea. The X factor is that we don't know *how many* of those twenty-four hour days we have. Look what Da Vinci accomplished during his life. Think what he might have accomplished if he'd had another 1,000 or 10,000 twenty-four hour time increments.

So, how can you unlock the secret of time? By *not* sleeping on it. In their 2015 "Sleep Duration Recommendations" chart, The National Sleep Foundation, a nonprofit research and advocacy group, suggests healthy adults between 18 – 64 years of age should get approximately seven to nine hours of sleep a night. If you change your sleep habit from eight to seven hours, you've just given yourself another 365 hours a year. Fifteen days. The X factor! This life hack helps maximize your productivity and gives you a distinct advantage over the sleepers. ("You snooze, you lose.")

Need more motivation? The National Sleep Foundation states that average mortality risk was higher for longer sleepers. University-based sleep research agrees, indicating that getting too much sleep is associated with health problems including diabetes and cardiovascular disease as well as with higher death rates. In recent sleep studies, the lowest rate of disease and mortality clocks in for those grabbing 7.2 hours of sleep.

Back in 2002, *The Journal of the American Medical Association* (JAMA), published an article* by (lead author) Daniel F. Kripke, an emeritus professor of psychiatry at the University of

California San Diego, that reported the results of a study in which 1.1 million people participated in a cancer study over a six year period. Participants who slept 6.5 to 7.4 hours had a lower mortality rate than those with shorter or longer sleep. (The study controlled for 32 health factors, including medications.)

Bottom line: Get enough sleep to stay healthy and creative, and save the big sleep for when you're dead.

* *Mortality Associated With Sleep Duration and Insomnia* – *JAMA Psychiatry*, February 2002, Vol 59, No. 2

"*The woods are lovely, dark and deep. But I have promises to keep, and miles to go before I sleep.*"

~ Robert Frost

Sometimes the best mousetrap is your mousetrap.

So, you have this unique, amazing idea that will forever change the world and earn you a mega-fortune in the process. Well, act now, before you Google it.

It can be both disheartening and motivating to find what you believed to be your sure-fire ticket to financial freedom, fame, and recognized genius already populating the first page of search results. Disheartening because someone beat you to it. Motivating because perhaps you are onto something.

If Monet hadn't painted because others had painted before him, if Steinbeck hadn't written because words had already succumbed to paper ... If that were the case we'd have but one song. One car. One sculpture. Heck, one shampoo—not dandruff reducing or with conditioner or split end remedy or frizzy hair or fine hair or oily hair ... just "shampoo"—because shampoo had already been invented. Why bother to improve on it or give it a new spin, right? Why, indeed.

If you don't take action on your desires simply because someone before you has done something similar, you're denying opportunities to engage your creativity and discover what it is that really motivates and nurtures you.

Deep down, you might simply be comparing yourself to others. You might think that others are smarter or better than you. Maybe you're thinking "why should you put my hat in the ring and be embarrassed?" Maybe you feel your creative spark is lesser than others.

Here's the thing: You don't have to re-invent something. Just make it *your* something. We all have unique abilities and individual vision. No one can see or imagine something *exactly* as you do. There is only one you, and whatever you do is uniquely yours. Will you create a better mousetrap and make bazillions of dollars? Maybe, maybe not. But you'll be exercising your imagination and ingenuity in your own style and doing what you love. You can't put a price tag on that.

"There's so many of them and only one of me!"

Exactly.

Hey mister, can you spare some change?

Gaze into a mirror and you'll find someone magical watching you. Someone no one else can ever be. You'll see not only who you are but all that you want to be, staring back at you, waiting for you to come alive.

Albert Einstein, when asked what he considered to be the most powerful force in the universe, answered: "Compound interest! What you have become is the price you paid to get what you used to want."

Take in the mirror's full picture. Not only will you see yourself, you'll see everything behind you as well. No matter where you go, turn around and there you were. You can change what you see behind you in the mirror by seeing how you envision your future in the mirror. The background will slowly change right along with you.

Okay, you can't change your past. But, you can choose who you are today and who you will be tomorrow. In this way, over time, you *are* changing who you were. You set the ground work for your current state by the choices you made in the past. If you want circumstances to change, change your thinking. Dream new dreams, set lofty goals, and work to make them your reality.

It's not so much self-help that is needed, but a resilient self-belief. Too many people wait for someone to tell them that they can create magic. To give them permission to dream. They look to coaches and counselors and clergy and cliques and pals. But few simply look into their mirror and discover for themselves that they *can.*

Writers are told to simply write about what they know. If that were true, we'd never have experienced Gulliver's Travels, Moby Dick, Harry Potter, or War of the Worlds. Fact is—if you can imagine it, dream it, and reach for it—who is to tell you, other than you, that you can't achieve it?

Irrepressible passion of self-belief is essential for an exuberant life. Sure, along the journey you're going to stumble and fall. And during those trying times, self-belief is the strongest gift of self-help that you will ever give yourself.

Perhaps you wouldn't want to change anything at all as you've led the perfect life. (If so, millions of people have been waiting for a couple thousand years for your return.) Point being, take the past—the good, the bad, and the middling—and use it to shape what you want today and in the future. What's in it for you? *Tomorrow.*

~ Whose permission do you need to live the life you want? ~
Hint: You'll find the answer in the mirror.

If it looks like a leopard and it sounds like a leopard, it's probably a leopard.*

You've probably heard the saying, "a leopard can't change his spots." This originated in the Bible, from *Jeremiah* 13:23 (King James Version), that states, "Can the Ethiopian change his skin, or the leopard his spots? Then may ye also do good, that are accustomed to do evil."

We aren't here to discuss religion though. For our purposes, let's focus on the basic premise of change.

As humans, and not the aforementioned leopards, we are quite capable of change. In some fashion or another we change a little bit every day of our lives—from the length of our fingernails and hair (or loss thereof) to the common sense, knowledge, skills, and abilities we acquire. We might change superficially (cosmetic surgery, Botox injections as example), physically (our nose and ears grow throughout life, and thanks to gravity, earlobes sag and noses droop), or mentally as we learn, adapt, and grow as individuals.

Sometimes we undergo drastic or dramatic changes, other times subtle—like a stone transformed by a steady river current. Change not easily noticed, but change nevertheless.

If you are seeking to create a change in your life and are willing to put in the work, you can make it happen. But change doesn't happen on its own. Simply wanting or longing for change in your life will only keep the status quo. If you want something, you have to get off your rear and do something about it.

Sure, it's easy, and often tempting, to do nothing. Unfortunately that's what you'll get in return. As an all-knowing, "the world owes me everything" teenager, my parents often said to me, "Why not just 'want' in one hand and crap in the other, and see which one fills first?"

Falling into a trap of believing that you can't do something, by people too scared to venture into their own life, is the real sin. But there are people out there that'll do it to you if you let them. Don't.

* You are not a leopard.

"*You don't see sick animals in the wild. You don't see lame animals in the wild, and it's all because of the predator: the lion, the tiger, the leopard, all the cats.*"
~ Tippi Hedren

Now what?

Ah, the anticipation for that day you leave worries behind, take some time for yourself, and do some exploring. Perhaps a leisurely walk or a challenging hike. Maybe a bike ride along a favorite trail, a sight-seeing car or motorcycle ride for a few hours.

Then it hits. You're two hours into this opportunity and you find yourself thinking, "Now what?" It happens. We've all been there. Can't wait to get some time to do something just for yourself, and then ... (insert sound of crickets chirping) ... nothing. And a back-up plan? Of course not. Everything was going to be perfect!

You can choose the day, the destination, and the route. Just about everything except the weather. But you can't force a good time. It's said when life hands you lemons, to make lemonade. What's not said is that without some sweetener and water, the lemonade is going to suck. Sometimes though, when things don't go as planned, they go exactly as they were intended.

Things won't always play out as they do in your head. That's okay. If everything smelled like roses you'd lose your appreciation for roses. It's discovering rarities that make adventure so alluring. Along the way, you'll endure your share of "Now what?" moments. Collect what you can from the experiences then tuck them away and move on. Life will, whether you do or not.

" What is really momentous and all-important with us is the present, by which the future is shaped and colored."

~ John Greenleaf Whittier

Running is futile, hiding impossible.

Remaining open and vulnerable is a challenge in a world where we are scrambling to feel safe and protected. There is so much bad news reported via so many outlets that it's easy to be numb to tragedy. It has become second nature to skim headlines, pausing at heartrending articles only long enough to see if it affects any place we've traveled, lived, or have friends or family.

The fact is, bad things happen, and pretending they won't or can't happen to you is naïve. Sure, getting bad news is a buzz-kill; ruining an otherwise perfectly good day. Life is fraught with misfortune and we inevitably shovel all that negativity onto our shoulders, carrying it around in a "woe is me" bindle, convincing ourselves that everyone else is living the life of Riley.

Take the time to read the news—good and bad. You'll learn what you already knew; that you aren't the only one out there. You'll also be better attuned to what's going on and better able to accept or adapt to life challenges while appreciating all the good that *does* come your way.

Turning a blind eye during difficult times won't solve a thing. If you stick your head in the sand, you'll just get shot in the ass. Head up, eyes open, one foot in front of the other. You're only beaten if you surrender.

"Sometimes you have to go through the ugly stuff to reach the prize. Learning to eat spaghetti was immortalized in photos by moms everywhere."

~ Michael

You are cleared for take-off.

One of the things that creates confusion in life is the internal picture of how we think it's supposed to play out. Now, with planning, hard work, self-belief, and dedication; dreams and goals are attainable. Along the way though, you are like an airplane with its attitude indicator going all over the place. Left, right, up, and down. You'll eventually find your landing strip, but it likely won't be a straight-shot from where you departed. (What fun would that be, anyway?)

We get this Mayberry vision and weigh those images against our reality, thus becoming our own worst enemy. It's okay to grab a sense of what or who you want to be from movies or books or neighbors or old TV shows. Those are fine places to capture ideas. But use them as that–ideas. Use the influences as a personal jumping off platform. Incorporate what you admire while making your life *yours*. Sure, at times, you will inevitably be your own worst enemy. So what. No one's perfect (see: the myth of perfection).

Here's a grand example–depending on which side of the conversation you are on–of putting yourself at the top of the pyramid and taking control of your life:

Some years ago I was present at a large technology company meeting being held at a downtown convention center. I was outside enjoying some fresh air when the company founder and CEO stepped out and fired up a cigarette. He stood quietly for a few minutes before turning towards me and launching the following observation, accompanied by a sweeping gesture at the city skyline. "You see all those buildings? The growth? Construction? The industry? The cash that fuels this economy?" I replied that I did. He continued, "Someday, if you work hard, diligently, relentlessly; ten, twelve, maybe sixteen hours a day, someday ..." then looking me square in the eyes finished, "... all this could be mine."

With that he dropped his cigarette to the ground, crushed it beneath his shoe, turned, and walked back into the convention center.

Lesson duly noted.

"Great news! The same person that installs your roadblocks can remove them. You."

~ Michael

Everyone's a critic these days.

The artist wants to be a builder. The builder wishes to be a pianist. The pianist thinks she should have studied archeology. Of course, these pursuits aren't exclusive of one another. At the end of the day, we chase what we enjoy, whether as vocation or hobby (or both). Still, many of us live shackled by mental chains that keep us from pursuing our aspirations because of a self-defeating tendency to compare ourselves to history's greats.

Okay, so maybe you'll never paint like Rembrandt. Why would you want to? He was an original. Just like you. Rembrandt was recognized for his talent because he was bold enough to put it out there for the world to experience. (And P.S.–Rembrandt could never paint like you either, lest he copied *your* style and technique.) If you escape from the encumbrance comparison, you'll find something else to fret about. Probably what other people will think of your composition, building, or painting. The dreaded critics.

When critics like our work, we think they are the smartest people alive. Brilliant spotters of talent! When they pan our work or critique it negatively, why, obviously they don't know what they're talking about. Look, critics are no smarter than the rest of us. In fact if Rembrandt hadn't painted because others might not like his work or because others had painted before him or if Shakespeare hadn't written because words had already been written ... If you *don't*, because someone else *has*—you are the one judging yourself to be inferior or unworthy. That, as the saying goes, is the worst critic of all.

While we're on the subject of critics, let's look at The Pavel Jerdanowitch Disumbrationism movement. In 1924, Los Angeles novelist Paul Jordan-Smith fooled the art world with this whopper. Sarah Bixby Smith, Jordan-Smith's wife, was a novice painter who had recently received a chilly review from jurors at a local art exhibition. This angered Jordan-Smith and he sought retribution by trying to prove that those critics wouldn't know good art from bad. He created, and assumed a double identity of a fictitious Russian painter he named Pavel Jordanowitch (a play on the name Paul Jordan).

Jordan-Smith stated, "I asked for paint and canvas and said I'd do a real modern—I'd never tried to paint anything in my life. Given the oldest tubes of red and green paint and a worn brush I took up a defective canvas and in a few minutes splashed out the crude outlines of an asymmetrical savage holding up what was intended to be a star fish, but turned out a banana. I labeled it 'Yes We Have No Bananas'."

In 1925, he entered the painting in New York's Exhibition of the Independents at the Waldorf-Astoria. He renamed it 'Exaltation,' and presented it as the work of his alter-ego, Russian artist Pavel Jerdanowitch.

Critics bit. Jordan-Smith received a letter from a French art journal, the *Revue du Vrai et du Beau* (Review of the True and the Beautiful), praising the work and requesting additional details. Smith wrote that it "represented the breaking of the shackles of womanhood" and concocted a tale to go along with it. This, along with Jerdanowitch's "biographical" information appeared in the next issue of the *Revue du Vrai et du Beau*, accompanied by critical acclaim. A legend was born.

Jordan-Smith continued this ruse into 1927, creating additional Pavel Jordanowitch works, receiving adoration and accolades until making a full confession to *Los Angeles Times* writer Alma Whitaker. The story of the hoax broke on the front page of the *LA Times* on August 14, 1927. Smith explained that he wanted to create spoofs to prove that much of the art in fashion was "poppycock" promoted by critics who knew little about art. He described the critics as "fraidy cats and poseurs."

The takeaway: Whatever you do, give it your best. If you're happy, you've succeeded. If you learn something, you've succeeded. Only by doing nothing do you fail.

"You're only as inferior as you allow yourself to be. Do what you love, and do it first and foremost, for yourself."

~ Michael

Decisions, decisions.

What do you do if you plant a garden so large that you can't tend to it by yourself? Well, for starters—congratulations. That's a marvelous dilemma! So, okay, let's take a look. You could plant a smaller garden, you could let part of a larger garden go to seed, or, you can share your garden with others. Grow big or grow alone.

It's said that we reap what we sow. Here, we're referring to making the conscious choice to plant your life garden with unlimited space; giving room for people and experiences to take root, foster, grow, and provide nourishment for your soul. Growing a life garden only large enough for yourself provides no room for roaming and discovery. While solitude has its rewards, it's more fulfilling when it's by choice. Of course, planting a generous life garden then allowing portions to die of neglect is as bad as planting (and thinking) small.

Grow a life so big that you leave nothing out. In a way, each of us is a living, breathing one person commune. It grows, supplements, supports, and nurtures our needs and does so best when our love, kindness, and compassion is shared with others— each of whom represent their own inner-commune. By seeking commonalities, we fill voids, find love, and harvest an ever-growing garden completing our life recipe; a simmering pot filled with special people and celebrated memories.

We all have needs and wants. We want to give or share something. The ritual of finding a like-minded person satisfies whatever emotion that forced its way to the top of your mental garden at the time. Sometimes when that specific need or desire is fulfilled, we go back to tending our garden. Other times we might have a need so strong or so basic and instinctual (or led by the considered norms of society) that we connect for longer duration, such as seeking a life partner or entering into marriage. Humans aren't alone in these endeavors. In some species of rats (specifically Malagasy Giant Rats of Madagascar), both parents stick around to raise the young. When one mate dies, the other will find a replacement, and widows often remain home in the burrow until a new suitor comes along. (*Scientific American*)

Lesson? Your life is a garden. You'll need patience, fertilizer (but don't overdo it; a little shit goes a long way), water (the inevitable tears will come), and strength to eliminate the weeds that creep into life before they take root (better a hoe than a sickle).

"The glory of gardening: hands in the dirt, head in the sun, heart with nature. To nurture a garden is to feed not just on the body, but the soul."

~ Alfred Austin

Your history is waiting.

Imagine for a moment that you are on a lush tropical island. You're relaxing on the beach. The air is warm as you watch the waves lash the shore. The sun beginning its descent. You have a book open, but you're not really reading. Instead, you look around, relaxed and daydreaming, watching others stroll by on the soft sand. A gorgeous afternoon.

Were you mentally on the beach for a few seconds? Unlike the environmental weather, we have the ability to control our own internal weather. It can rain, snow, create unbearable heat, or a nice tropical breeze. Your call. You don't have to splash around someone else's grumpy-storm. It begins in *your* head, not theirs. Don't buy into someone else's weather report.

Keep an open mind. Recognize opportunity when presents itself, and when you get tired of waiting, go look for it! You don't know what you don't yet know. Metaphorically speaking, if you don't take risks or have faith in yourself, you'll never know if stepping over the edge of the cliff means you can actually fly. It's your autobiography and each day is a page of your history waiting to be written.

"*Either write something worth reading or do something worth writing.*"

~ Benjamin Franklin

Happy birthday!

The past, present, and life's future are inter-related. Anniversaries, birthdays, holidays, and graduations—life events of times past and times yet to come.

We reminisce with loved ones and celebrate those special occasions over and again through photos and videos. What do they have in common? They are all past events. We spend huge amounts of mental energy reliving the past.

Perhaps we cherish those times because we don't know what the future holds. We tempt fate every day in different, singular ways (oh, how boring otherwise). Because of that, we have a tendency to fall back on the tried and true—happy memories from the past, remembrances, and traditions born ages ago.

Unfortunately, we spend so much time celebrating the past we often neglect celebrating *today* (without celebrating the past in the process) and creating something that others will enjoy in the future. Enjoy memories of the past, but don't leave your own legacy in a dusty attic. Live in the present, make future memories, and build your own photo and video playlists.

" *The best part of today isn't yesterday. Or tomorrow. It's today.*

Live in it."

~ Michael

Life Lessons From:

- **Bigfoot**–No matter how big and strong you are, sometimes it's wise to keep quiet and stay out of sight.
- **Dentists**–A smile is one of your best assets.
- **Magicians**–Seeing may be believing, but doesn't make it true. Question everything.
- **Sushi**–Things can go bad quickly if you overstay your welcome.
- **Dogs**–Distance and time are states of mind. Gone five minutes or five days? Who knows. It doesn't matter when you truly love someone.
- **Superman** –No matter how strong or invincible, you have your kryptonite.
- **Shovels**–Whether it's snow or bullshit, no matter how much you remove, there'll always be more.
- **Guillotine**–No matter how sharp you are, not everyone is going to like you. Get over it, not under it.
- **Ass**–Everyone has one or is one. Often both.
- **Mime**–Sometimes it pays to keep your mouth shut.
- **Airplanes**–No matter how high or fast you fly, you'll eventually land.
- **Toilets**–Shit happens and someone has to be at the bottom to deal with it.
- **Death**–There isn't always going to be a tomorrow. Live today.

Focus, focus, focus.

Here are a few words that keep the antacids in the medicine cabinet: Focus on solutions, not problems. The problem is the lesser of issues. Not focusing on the solution is the bigger problem.

Consider this example (and the potential ramifications) of focusing on perceived problems and not the solution: Those with a fear of doctors (iatrophobia) may not be inclined to be honest and open with their health care providers because they are worried their ailment might be a symptom of a serious disease. This is ironic, because only by being forthright will there be opportunity for treatment. Either way, there are only a few options: they'll be okay or they won't. Those options narrow to the negative when a person chooses to be reticent with their care provider. The person will both heal and be fine or they may discover that they do have a serious disease which, left untreated, could have grim consequences. The choice (to be open and honest) seems a no-brainer, yet there are scores of people that keep the information to themselves, and in some instances, literally die from their fear.

If your house was on fire; calling 911 and getting your family to safety would come instinctively. But when it comes to life decisions, too often we just sit around waiting for problems to miraculously resolve on their own. A personal gaper's block. We can't help but stare. In doing so, we are not helping direct traffic or rescuing people trapped in cars. It's likely we're compounding the problem, slowing or blocking traffic, and impeding rescue workers (who *are* taking action).

We get so engulfed in the flames that we forget to grab a fire extinguisher. Assess the problem, digest available information, use your common sense, and take action. Knowing you make the best decision you can, with the information you have, is better than sitting on your thumbs waiting for someone to solve your problems for you. And believe you me; there are plenty of people out there that will gladly run your life for you if you let them.

It's like telling yourself you need to lose fifteen lbs. (or five or five-hundred) and get in better shape. You think about it, you check weight management sites, you research health club costs, you read food labels in the stores, you observe others in similar situations, and you watch reality weight loss shows. You even buy a book or two on healthy eating. Okay, you've identified the problem. Check. You are armed with sufficient information to do something about it. Check. But you don't take action. Again, the problem is often the lesser of issues. Not focusing on the solution and following-up with tangible action is the larger problem.

So, what's your excuse for not tackling an important life issue? You don't want to solve the problem, you're scared to solve the problem, you're afraid of being hurt, of hurting someone, of change, of being wrong, or messing up, of embarrassing yourself, you don't have the time, your mom/dad/husband/wife/neighbor/co-worker/ friends/church/bus driver wouldn't approve, you don't have the money, no transportation, no ... no ... no ...? You see, there is always an easy excuse to do nothing. Always.

It's an old (but accurate) saying, "a journey of a 1,000 miles begins with a single step." You put one foot in front of the other and keep going. You're not likely to just awake some morning thinner, richer, happier, prettier, or healthier. It won't happen until *you* take action to make it happen. Baby steps. Given time, even babies will cover tremendous ground and will grow and stride longer, faster, and more confidently each day.

Stop sitting. Start crawling, and then learn to walk again. Now. Seriously, now.

" The biggest mistake you can make is being afraid to make one."

~ Michael

Victory in inches.

It's impossible to solve a problem without first identifying it. As I like to say, "For the truth, don't look at the color of the hair—look for the color of the roots."

Then there's that venerable adage, "It's not the destination it's the journey." But, the journey is greatly enriched if you visualize a destination. For instance, professionally you might enjoy working a variety of jobs with no particular focus other than food, shelter, and clothing. But that also comes with an anchor: food, clothing, and shelter (in this case, an abstract destination). If you work without basic necessities in mind—well, that's called an internship, but I digress. But even unpaid interns aren't working without purpose. They acquire peripheral experience anticipating that their education and newfound practical knowledge will catapult them into a desirable position. While a whimsical, nomadic lifestyle may sound somehow freeing and romantic, it probably ain't gonna pay the bills.

So, back to square one. The tight wire act of fulfilling basic needs while discovering the journey leading to your undeniable destination. Keep in mind that your destination doesn't have to be a physical place. Your destination may truly be that nomadic life. And your journey—working and creating it—is the destination. Sometimes the journey and the destination intertwine.

There are numerous resources to help give you a jumpstart. You might look into the *Law of Attraction* (multiple titles) or Barbara Sher and Annie Gotlieb's *Wishcraft*. Still, it begins with knowing what you want to—what you *will*—achieve in life. As Yogi Berra is credited with saying, "If you don't know where you are going, you might wind up someplace else." I'm not sure that's such a bad idea though. After all, if you don't discover what you don't like, how will you appreciate what you do cherish when you find it?

Once you discover your destination, things fall into line. It might not be a huge Aha! revelation. You'll need to do some consistent digging and chipping away. Ranch hand, soldier, merchant marine, poet, and acclaimed Western author, Louis L'Amour, put it like this: "Victory is won not in miles but in inches. Win a little now, hold your ground, and later, win a little more."

The sooner you get off your rear and get started, the sooner you'll reach the destination (perhaps the first of many) that's out there waiting for you. It's always the right time to weigh anchor and set sail.

"To reach a port we must sail, sometimes with the wind, and sometimes against it. But we must not drift or lie at anchor."
~ Oliver Wendell Holmes

The sun is always out.

How about those days where it seems like no matter where you are or what you're doing or who you're with (even alone!), everything just rubs you the wrong way or pisses you off. Yeah, those.

Last summer I was in a peaceful neighborhood park talking with a friend who was having a particularly rough day of things. It was a beautiful, picture perfect setting. During a pause in conversation a nearby song bird chirped its melody as the sun splashed through the branches. My friend looked up and said, "I don't know what the hell it's so happy about!"

Of course, if you're looking to find something *wrong*, you'll inevitably find it. We all have those days. And that's okay. Sometimes you just need to get it out of your system rather than bring it home with you. Look for the good. It's out there and is much more beneficial for your mental and physical health than expecting the frustrating and dreary. Here's a personal story with a succinct and delightful example of someone seeking the positive:

Many years ago, I worked at a large urban medical center. After work one day, I was walking across the sky bridge with one of the Catholic Sisters. I casually commented on the dreary weather and charcoal gray skies, saying "I wish the sun would come out." She punched my right bicep and admonished, "The sun is out; you're just not looking for it."

That observation has remained with me for many years and I think about it every now and again when I need a change in attitude. I tell myself, *"You control your weather. The sun is out."*

One more related note: I've also learned the hard way that it pays to find the source of what's gnawing at you. I've found that it's not always the who or the when that need to be examined, but the what and the why. As example, that Aiden cracked a window on Saturday may not be nearly as important as the fact that the window is cracked and why. Often, answering the latter also answers the former, but seldom the other way round.

Everything for a reason. Learn the reason.

"When you rise in the morning, give thanks for the light, for your life, for your strength. Give thanks for your food and for the joy of living. If you see no reason to give thanks, the fault lies in yourself."

~ Tecumseh

"I'm thankful for all the weeds in my garden."

There. I said it. And I mean it, too! I am thankful for those weeds. Thankful for the satisfaction I feel once I've yanked them out and for the clarity and beauty that remains. And I know that their inevitable return will provide another opportunity to experience those feelings of accomplishment over and again. This is no different than waxing a car or painting a room or creating a great meal. Achievement, pride, and satisfaction. Rather than get too bummed out over the weeds (mind you, I didn't say that I want to *grow* weeds), I give myself a pat on the back for the achievement and for the opportunity it gives to celebrate the accomplishment.

If pulling weeds doesn't provide a sense of accomplishment—fine—don't pull them. Go au naturel. Or how about contributing to the community by hiring a few neighborhood kids to do it for you? Weeds grow like ... well, weeds. You can cuss them, kill them, or burn them. They'll come back and there's always more than enough to go around.

Weeds have a lot in common with rain. You don't want the skies to open up just after you wash and wax your car because it looks great and you put in considerable time and effort to make it shine. Well, rain is just Mother Nature's way of giving you another opportunity to experience that pride all over again. That and weeds. Lots of weeds.

"If food brought true happiness we'd only need to eat once."

~ Michael

Excluded or simply not included?

Being excluded from a get-together is an ego-bruising experience. Friends going out without you, co-workers getting together on a Friday afternoon after a long week.

Consider this: Perhaps you weren't excluded. Maybe you simply were not *included*. With the former, a conscious decision was made to omit you from the activity. In the latter, you were never part of the conversation. That's where our overwhelming need for acceptance plays havoc with our emotions.

There could be many reasons why you might be excluded; others didn't think you'd enjoy yourself, the situation wasn't appropriate, or maybe they were going to a club and you don't drink or dance. Myriad things could create a circumstance where you might be excluded. Not all of which are necessarily negative, but conscious thought *was* used in making the decision. (You might not have wanted to participate anyway—but resented not being asked.)

Not being *included* is an altogether different animal than simply being excluded. Not being included comes with the premise that you *were* considered but not invited—perhaps to an activity you would really have enjoyed. So, why would you not be included? That's the million-dollar question. Each situation has its own circumstances, but you can usually get to the bottom of this little mystery fairly quick. I don't have the answer, but I know who does; the people who chose not to invite you. I'm a big proponent of taking a direct—yet tactful—approach, so, I'll tell you the same thing I'd tell anyone else. If you're dealing with friends, *ask*. If they are your friends they'll tell you. Caveat—don't ask if you don't want to hear their response.

Sure, that's easier said than done, but do you want to carry around all that resentment? It will grow till you're never invited to anything, period.

If asking doesn't work for you, consider having your own get-together and see who makes the effort to attend. I'm sure you'll find some interesting parallels. At the end of the day, wouldn't you rather be excluded than not included?

"I don't know what I've done more of in life—made friends or lost friends. But I know I tried hard at one and probably nudged the other a bit as well."
~ Michael

Zip it. Nada. Zilch. Shut up.

Once you've achieved agreement or reached a truce with another person—whether in intellectual debate or fierce argument—it's time to shut up. When you get what you want or if you realize (and are wise enough to admit) that the other person is correct; zip it.

Keep talking and you'll find yourself right back at square one. The damage is exponentially exacerbated when you insist on trying to prove how right you are when the other party has already nodded agreement. You move from a place of being a valid information resource to just being a blow-hard know-it-all. Stop talking. Likewise, if the other party has made valid points (even if—especially if—contradictory to your stance), acknowledge it and move on. Who needs more enemies? Learn to win both the battle *and* the war.

Here's another tip: When words fail you, perhaps you think yelling is the only option to make your point or to be heard. But yelling at someone doesn't increase their comprehension. The only thing you are certain to achieve is making the person less, not more, inclined to listen to you when you are whispering. That and it'll piss them off. Shut up, already.

"*Lower your voice and strengthen your argument.*"

~ Lebanese proverb

Speaking of not speaking.

The next time you are so angry with someone that your eyes are bleeding, so frustrated you want to rip out your hair—remember: there is a remedy. A magical solution guaranteed to bring you back to center.

Here's your magic: *Do nothing.* Do nothing, write nothing. Try, "I need to think about this," or, "give me ten minutes." Then take a walk and gather your thoughts. Come from a position of strength and logic, not anger or frustration. Acting out of frustration is self-feeding. The next problem, the next challenge, the next piss-off, is always on its way.

In conflict, there are two matters in play: the issue and the emotions. Separate the two and tackle them separately. Address the emotional aspects first (this is where doing nothing and stepping away for a few minutes to sort it all out comes into play). The other person likely knows (or is quickly learning) what your hot buttons are and how to push them. They may try to provoke you and further drag you into an argument. Stay calm and weather the storm. Engaging—especially if your goal is to try and prove someone wrong—simply fuels the fire.

It's usually not one huge moment or singular action that brings about a crisis. It's typically a cumulative effect with each conflict building on the last, creating a venomous cycle. Individually, it may not be enough to break a heart or ruin a relationship, but each slash is a small tear, baring a little more with each rip, making it easier to tear in the future till it simply folds and collapses under its own weight. Recognize. Stop. Sew. Mend. Heal.

Here's another tip: If the clash is online and you're keying so fast your Wi-Fi is melting, put your device down. Responding in anger is like drunk dialing: it's never a good idea. Even when you're certain of the brilliance of your prose—don't hit send. If what you have to say is relevant, it will still be relevant once you've calmed down. In these instances, nothing = everything.

"Speak when you are angry–and you'll make the best speech you'll ever regret."

~ Laurence J. Peter

Decisions and choices.

How do you balance personal principles or needs with relationship challenges? As example, let's say you are highly allergic to cats. You've met this great guy and your first date is going well. After lunch, the two of you are talking about work and life interests— just idle chat. It's then that you learn that this great guy has two cats, volunteers at an animal shelter, and works full-time as a pet sitter. You have a dilemma.

While you admire this person's loving and selfless approach to life, you can't be near him or his home without succumbing to a daily pill regiment or periodic injections. As a rule, you take a holistic approach to life and healing. Is this a doable situation or a deal breaker?

Are "deal breakers" and "principles" necessarily the same? If you are a liberal, can you live with a staunch conservative? Does it matter? Should it matter? Would it create discourse or provide stimulating conversation? Would you celebrate the differences or want to rip each other's eyes out?

Robyn Roybal, a marketing manager in Bellevue, WA, believes that it comes down to an individual's belief system, saying "I think it depends more on how strong a person's beliefs are and how accepting and open-minded they are to other people's beliefs."

Another friend describes it this way, "Look at the religious wars fought in this world. Do you think you could ever change their minds, or have them be accepting of a spouse with a different religious belief? Not a chance." He continued, "On the other hand my dad was raised as a strict catholic, was an altar boy, still regularly attends church, and has been married for nearly forty years to my step-mom who doesn't even believe a god exists. They make it work."

Roybal added, "I also know a couple who got together with the woman having two cats (and a dog) and her partner was extremely allergic. In the end the cats were given away, they moved in together, and eventually married. They also found a new home for the dog. On the other hand, I would probably let my partner go before I gave my dog away."

As these examples demonstrate, where there's a will there's a way, but only if both parties are flexible and open to compromise. At the end of the day, it comes down to just about what you might imagine. Open, honest conversation. How do you balance this in your life?

"It's not that you have to make a decision, it's that you get a choice."

~ Michael

Solving For X.

Remember those tedious (for many of us) math quizzes, when producing the answer wasn't enough? You also had to "show your work," demonstrating proof of understanding the process required to reach a successful solution.

Showing your work is how the teacher knows that you understand the problem. It's a vital form of communication, just like speaking or writing. Showing that you can effectively communicate in a given language (algebra, trigonometry, BASIC, COBOL, et al) makes it easier to share ideas with your peers. For instance, in a math class, it's common to hear, "How did you get that answer?" Showing your work is a communication tool. It's the math equivalent of using nouns, verbs, subject, and predicate to create a sentence.

Some might ask, "Why do I have to show my work if I've reached the correct solution?" Sure, you can probably do some (or even most) of the steps in your head and arrive at the correct answer. But this is where problems can creep in. Working it out in your head without knowing the steps can cause you to reach the same, perhaps *erroneous*, answer time and again. If your goal is to consistently reach a productive, accurate conclusion, it helps to know how you got there. If you become stumped, you'll probably ask someone for help. But, if they can't see the work you've done to get where you are, they might not be able to help you find the correct answer. Saying, "I just figured it out in my head," doesn't provide much of a roadmap.

You'll make mistakes. The goal is to isolate them, correct them, and not make the same error again. Sound familiar? You guessed it. Life works much the same way. You can get lucky a time or two, but knowing how you fail or succeed helps you learn and build on those results. You can replicate, improve, change, discard, or repeat as desired. And, since knowledge is seldom used in a vacuum, learnings are useful throughout life. We use what we know to learn more about what we don't.

Know your work to better show your work.

~ Do the math. Learn the lessons. ~

Heather, please stop barking!

My next door neighbor was spreading fresh bark along the south edge of his front yard, dressing up spring anticipating summer's arrival. Our property line was a vague, unseparated intersection of approximately three feet. The neighbor, whom I'd met only a few times, courteously and generously laid bark across his property line and extended it the entire three feet so that there was no sudden and silly looking empty lane of dirt abutting the colorful bark.

Unbeknownst to him, my other half had previously decided that the area would look great lined with heather plants. She wanted to create a free growing, elongated floral bloom area, so she raked the edge of fresh bark back onto the neighbor's property and planted nursery-fresh heather. While my other half is pleased with her work, I'm curious if our neighbor wondered if we felt trespassed by his desire to be, well ... *neighborly*.

Everyone had intentions of creating an aesthetic landscape. This goal was achieved and it looks great. Even so, my significant other wondered why the neighbor shoveled bark on our property and our neighbor might have wondered why we didn't seem appreciate his generous gesture.

This reminded me of a cartoon strip I'd seen showing two separate groups building a cross-country railroad from west to east and east to west, meant to join in the middle, only to be off by three feet. In the final panel, the cartoon characters were depicted standing around scratching their heads and pointing at each other wondering how the other group could have so egregiously erred.

In both the yard situation and the fictional railroad scenario, a little open communication could have avoided any misunderstanding. Even when everyone has great intentions, a little communication goes a long way. Be clear about your desires and intentions—both to others *and* to yourself. If you don't speak up to be heard, you're giving up a valid claim to criticize.

It's easier to create something than to change other's opinion of it once it's done. Communication and compromise.

"The most important trip you may take in life is meeting people halfway."

~ Henry Boye

Life requires a beautiful frame.

An attractive frame draws interest to the photo or art that it is tasked with displaying. It affects how we perceive what it contains. How we see the frame contributes to how we view what is contained in the frame. Choosing just the right frame for a given display piece is important and reflects the personal style or both the art and the framer.

You might come across a piece of art you like—perhaps at a yard sale, boutique, or art fair—but do not like the frame. You bring the art home and go about finding a suitable frame that best displays the piece. You reframe it to create the image you want to see, then proudly display it for all.

We do the same thing in other areas of life as well. Reframing how you feel about something can have considerable impact on how you experience it. Reframing refers to changing how you view ideas and emotions. As example, instead of having a fear of the unknown, you see it as a curiosity. You're more likely to try something new if you're curious about it rather than afraid of it. On the surface, reframing seems inherently simple. However, it requires a willingness to be open to fresh schools of thought and to tackle internal obstacles with creative thinking.

If you've always been afraid of the dark, it won't come natural or be easy to sit in a dark room. It's work. Maybe you add music. Maybe you use a flashlight every few minutes to assure yourself you're safe. You're seeking to overcome the fear or obstacle or event. You're mentally attempting to *reframe* the experience in a way your mind will recognize at as positive or, at least, inert and harmless.

206

So, how do you go about reframing? Step one: Focus on positive outcomes. Work to eliminate negative connotations (instead of sitting in the dark wondering about spiders and zombies and ghosts; concentrate on the peace, solitude, and reflective thinking time you have). Step two: Be bold. Be curious. Ask questions. Don't ruminate that you can't see because the room is dark. Think instead about your tactile senses—smell, touch, and sound. Mentally *reframe* the situation. Seek answers, knowing you'll never have all of them. And that's okay. Sometimes curiosity is its own reward. Once you are *curious* about the dark, you'll find as many opportunities waiting there as there are in daylight.

*(**Note**: You can learn more about reframing or cognitive therapies by reading the works of American psychiatrist Aaron T. Beck.)*

"My life has been filled with terrible misfortunes, most of which have never happened."

~ Mark Twain

Was that an earthquake?

Good vibrations, written by Brian Wilson and Mike Love, and recorded by the Beach Boys in 1966, has an interesting origin. Wilson was asked its meaning, speculation being that it was a drug-infused jam session. To the contrary, he described how his mother (and Mike Love's aunt), Audree Wilson, described to him why dogs bark at some people and not others. "A dog would pick up vibrations from these people that you can't see but you can feel. And the same thing happened with people. Good Vibrations harnessed that energy and turned it into eternal sunshine. This is a very spiritual song," Wilson said, "and I want it to give off good vibrations."

The concept of vibrations in life is not new, from science to metaphysical belief to stock market investing. Consider:

Controversial investor William Delbert Gann (1878–1955), was either a misguided blow-hard or a brilliant trader and stock speculator, depending on who and what you believe. One of the tools he developed was based on vibrations.

Gann said that stock prices have a way of repeating themselves—or "vibrating." Gann stated, "Through the law of vibration, every stock and commodity in the market place moves in its own distinctive sphere of activities, as to intensity, volume and direction. All the essential qualities of its evolution are characterized in its own rate of vibration. Vibration is fundamental; nothing is exempt from its law. It is universal, therefore, applicable to every class of phenomena on the globe. Thus, I affirm, every class of phenomena whether in nature or in the markets, must be subject to the universal laws of causation, harmony and vibration." (traderslog.com)

The Law of Vibration is one of the Universal Laws typically associated with new age beliefs, and includes such well-known theories as the Law of Attraction (search your favorite bookseller and you'll find a plethora of books on this topic).

The Law of Vibration states that everything in the universe moves, vibrates, and travels in circular patterns. There is a vibration in all living things, and the rate of vibration determines its form. Slow vibration manifests as a rock, fast vibration registers as wind, very high vibrations as sound and music. (mindinsync.com)

Stereo speakers are also a good example. A speaker's paper cone vibrates, creating the sound we hear with our ears. An alternating current (i.e., electrical audio signal input) is directed through a voice coil (Faraday's law *), causing the cone attached to the coil to respond with a back-and-forth motion, creating sound waves.

Those sound waves travel through the outer ear and are transmitted to a nerve in the inner ear where a nerve transmits information to the brain, where it is registered as ... ta daaaa ... sound. Sound that travels through the outer ear impacts our ear drum causing it to—you guessed it—vibrate. (Or, in lay terms, that car next to you at the traffic light, rattling your windows with their bass system.)

Physics gets in on the act as well. In 1984, two physicists, Michael Green (Queen Mary College) and John Schwarz (California Institute of Technology) published a paper on string theory that challenged long-accepted principles of physics. Messrs. Green and Schwarz hypothesized that subatomic particles contain a vibrating, string-like filament and that the difference between one particle and another is the difference in how their strings vibrate. These vibrations are what give rise to the different properties of quarks and atoms. Similar to how guitars and other string instruments produce sound through the vibration of their strings, the different particles can be considered the notes comprising nature's musical score. Good vibrations, indeed!

Coming full circle, people—and certainly our canine companions—can usually "feel" a person (or "sound them out") about how they might mesh or clash in their life. Perhaps we should listen to our dog rather than telling it what to do. Of course, that would mean most mail carriers are giving off bad vibrations. Then again, it could just be the stack of bills they are getting ready to stuff into the mail box.

For inquisitive readers, (Michael) Faraday's law states, "the induced electromotive force in any closed circuit is equal to the negative of the time rate of change of the magnetic flux through the circuit."

~ Ask yourself: *"Am I sending out good vibrations?"* ~

Will they be able to pick you out of a line-up?

For most people, the further removed from something they become, the less factually they recall it. As example, you probably remember what you had for dinner last night, but how about lunch two weeks ago Thursday? No calendar peeking!

Our legal system provides abundant evidence of the potential pitfalls wrought by relying on memory recall. While eye witness testimony is often used in criminal cases, its reliability has long been open to question. Of the 21 cases on The Innocence Network's* 2011 exoneration report, 19 wrongful convictions involved eyewitness testimony. This is consistent with statistics that indicate more than three-quarters of convictions later overturned by DNA evidence relied on faulty eyewitness evidence. This is nothing new. For his 1932 book, *Convicting the Innocent*, Yale law professor Edwin Borchard studied 65 wrongful convictions and found that eyewitness misidentification was the leading cause of wrongful convictions.

But in our personal lives? Of course there's no faulty memory! Those were the good old days! You know, everyone was blissful, birds chirped their happy songs under a sapphire sky, streams were tap-water clear and chock full of fish fighting for space, and all jobs paid beaucoup bucks. Aah. The good old days.

Funny how that works. If it's something you're not emotionally attached to though, say, a past job, you probably don't have any problem whatsoever remembering how much of a jerk the boss was, how you were underpaid, or how much the hours sucked. But you sure do miss some of your co-workers. Maybe even stay in touch with a few. So—the job sucked. The people, maybe not so much. Why aren't they intertwined? Because our brains do a fantastic job of siloing, categorizing, and filing. Job = suck. Tom, down the hall = cool guy. Even though Tom was part of a sucky workplace.

And oh, that boss. You know—the jerk. His Achilles' heel is forgetting the path that took him to the throne. While it's good to be king, it would be smart to know what the rest of the realm is up to. The boss doesn't have to be able to perform every job in the company, but better well recognize its purpose, significance, and place in the organization. The further you climb up the professional ladder, the more likely it is that you will grow out of touch with day-to-day workplace realities. I challenge the CEO of any Fortune 100 company to show me how to copy, staple, collate, or bind a document.

The sense of entitlement seems to grow on the ascent. Memories fade and expectations that stuff just magically happens take hold. And, surprise, stuff usually does get done. But not because the king demands it. It gets done for personal reasons. Either the person doing the work needs the income (and perks that might come with it), or they hold strong convictions about what they are doing and a fervent belief in the mission (volunteering is a prime example). The reason is in there, lurking. Ain't no one gonna wax your car for you just because they're bored.

In our personal lives, we tend to think that absence makes the heart grow fonder, but only because we're apt to reminisce about the good stuff and rationalize the remainder. No one remembers the work. We forget the fears, the tears, the longings, and the heartache. Depending on how you see it, selective memory is either one of life's great gifts or a cruel mistress.

Further thickening the fog, we remember things as we choose, not always as they were. History is written and rewritten every day. And unlike 5,000 years ago where we have perhaps only a sole accounting, we now have thousands of armchair historians regularly chiming in with their version of history. Including yours. And mine.

Bottom line: We see and remember what we want to see and remember. Live your life in a way that sets you apart from the ordinary. Give someone a reason to remember you in a way that is impossible to do without a smile. That's where the surprising magic lives.

* The Innocence Network is an affiliation of organizations that provides pro bono legal and investigative services to individuals seeking to prove their innocence of crimes for which they have been convicted and working to redress the causes of wrongful convictions.
(www.theinnocencenetwork.org)

"Images fade with time and we repaint them with our imagination."

~ Michael

So, you made a decision.

You did the right thing. You know you did. You weighed all available information, considered all sides of the challenge, turned it upside down, inside out, and rattled it to see if anything came loose. You made a sound decision based on solid information and pulled the proverbial trigger. Whew. That was tough. Very, very tough.

Now comes the "what the heck did I do," second guessing. Searching for the courage to trust in your decision. The ability to put it to bed and let it be. Here are a few things to keep in mind:

- You'll never be perfect. You will make mistakes. Everyone does.
- Trust yourself. Make the best decision you can with the information you have.
- Don't beat yourself up if the outcome isn't what you wanted. Live to live another day. You'll get another shot.

Second guessing and hindsight have one thing in common—they live in the past. Grasp the learnings of the past, use that knowledge to guide your future, and most of all—trust in yourself. Sleep will come.

"Between an idea and a deed stands procrastination. At some point you have to do something."

~ Michael

Do you smell that?

You can't see it. But you sure can sense it. Something brewing. Your mind is telling you something that you can't yet quite put your hands around. A harbinger.

Before rain begins, one of the first clues that it's on the way is that unmistakable chlorine-like, pungent scent. Ozone. Ozone's odor is detectable by many people at concentrations as little as 10 parts per billion (ppb) in the air.

Once the rain hits? That's Petrichor; the instantly recognized scent of rain on earth. (It comes from oils given off by vegetation and released into the air.) So, the next time you find yourself saying that it "smells like rain," trust your gut. You're probably right. You might not know the specific *why* or *when*, but you know the *what*.

Your instincts—your intuition—gets better as you rack up life experiences. The more you know about something, the easier it is to trust your gut. Some things are common sense, others not so much. But the scent is always there. When we trust our gut on something, we're accessing our subconscious, searching for similar situations or related feelings. For instance, if you're hiring someone, you'll check their references, but you'll also trust your instincts. You might not be able to specifically explain what it is that caused you to make a hiring decision, but your *gut* likely played a role in the process. Sometimes you'll be wrong (like the twelve publishers who told J.K. Rowling that *Harry Potter* was unsellable). It happens. But better to get it wrong on your terms.

Intuition is one of the things that separates humans from computers. Computers make decisions based on facts and information we input. As humans, we don't always have all the facts, and thus, we rely on our experiences, feelings, and ... instinct. Computers don't have a gut. They play strictly by the numbers.

It's valuable to recognize when you're acting from intuition and when your actions are coming from a place of fear. For instance, common sense tells you not to stick your hands into an open flame. Intuition might tell you not to get a ride home from carload of strangers. It might be fear telling you not to take skydiving lessons. (Sure, it can be intuition or common sense—each action or potential scenario can have multiple factors.)

The goal is to act based on knowledge, common sense, and a bit of intuition, while not being so controlled by fear that you miss out on life. Feelings of fear often manifest as instinct. "I'm not going into that dark room—there's broken glass on the floor." Your instincts are warning you that you might be injured. Other times fear manifests as imagination; "I'm not going into that dark room—it's filled with zombies and goblins." Intuition is based on past feelings and emotions. We know instinctively that fire will burn. But it's simple fear and imagination that a darkened room is filled with zombies and goblins. This loops back to gaining life experience. The more we experience life, the better our instincts. The more you know, the sharper your spidey senses. When you smell the ozone, the Petrichor can't be far behind.

"*Things are seldom entirely as they appear. Before the final reckoning, we're all led astray.*"

~ Michael

Give me a moment.

Preparing for what has yet to come makes it difficult to live in the present. Of course, living in the present is hard because as soon as we do, it's part of the past. Fortunately—we do have some say in this time conundrum.

Our present actions affect the course and potential outcomes of future endeavors. In any case, while living in the present we still tend to keep an eye on the close future that we're tailgating. (In fact, we just passed that one.)

As esoteric as it may seem, it's more suitable to consider ourselves as living in the *moment*—rather than in the present. Because it's either never or always the present. It can't be both. We are in a perpetual cycle of change.

Consider the arrow paradox (also known as fletcher's paradox), authored by Greek philosopher Zeno of Elea. The paradox states, *"If everything when it occupies an equal space is at rest, and if that which is in locomotion is always occupying such a space at any moment, the flying arrow is therefore motionless."* It cannot move to where it is not, because no time elapses for it to move there; it cannot move to where it is, because it is already there. In other words, at every instant of time there is no motion occurring. If everything is motionless at every instant, and time is entirely composed of instants, then motion is impossible. This argument rests on an assumption of plurality: that time is composed of moments (or "nows").*

The past, like a roller coaster, was fun, scary, enlightening, sometimes regrettable, and always memorable. But you can't drive forward by navigating via the rear-view mirror. (And don't look over your shoulder because you are perpetually gaining on yourself!) Eyes ahead. Adapt and prepare. Even as you are reading this, change is happening around you. As English naturalist and geologist Charles Darwin is credited with saying, "It is not the strongest of the species that survive, nor the most intelligent, but the one most responsive to change."

* For readers interested in learning more, check your local library or search online for Zeno's Paradox or Paradoxes of Motion.

"Change. A small, six letter word that electrifies us, scares the shit out of us, or both."
~ Michael

No one cares about you, like you.

A few other treasure hunters and I were poking around a neighborhood garage sale a while back, flipping through old albums and dusty paperbacks when a man abruptly said—loud enough for the few of us there to hear—"this stuff sucks!" He then turned and purposefully traipsed off. The woman conducting the sale never took her eyes off the man's back as he climbed into his car. She immediately went into defense mode, wondering aloud what his problem was and explaining to no one in particular how she carefully laid everything out, had a wide selection with something for everyone, and now just felt like tossing everything into boxes and calling it a day.

We have all behaved similarly (to each of them) at one time or another. He believed that he'd wasted time and she felt slighted by a stranger. The very ordinariness of the interaction is what made it interesting to observe.

It wasn't as though he jetted into town to check out a high-end estate auction, and she certainly wasn't proffering Tiffany lamps or Fabergé eggs. Even so, emotions were heightened. It didn't need to be a huge deal to create hurt feelings, disappointment, or frustration. To the contrary, it's often the small stuff that sets us off. In the case of the lady running the garage sale, she was practically giving items away (in fact, had a box filled with "free" things), selling stuff that held little or no personal or monetary value to her, yet she took it personal because, to her, it was rejection. "Doesn't like my stuff, ergo, doesn't like me." It wasn't the money or the stuff. It was the dismissal and the hurt feelings that came along with it.

The lesson here is to separate yourself from the material object and the situation. It wasn't about her. It was that some unknown person didn't want stuff that, frankly, she didn't want either. Successful salespeople learn this lesson early and often. Overcoming rejection. And rejection takes on many forms. From someone not wanting your stuff at a garage sale to not getting a job you were perfect for, to not winning the lottery. Those experiencing success in their professional and personal lives recognize that rejection is to be expected and they keep putting one foot in front of the other.

Thomas Edison said, "I have not failed. I've just found 10,000 ways that won't work." This is true in all life endeavors. Writing is another example. Just because an article or book proposal might be rejected numerous times, doesn't mean the writer is a bad person. The rejecter simply doesn't want, or care for, or need that material at that specific time. Successful salespeople (and writers) develop Teflon skin and don't take rejection personally.

J.K. Rowling's initial Harry Potter manuscript was rejected by twelve publishing houses before getting the green light. Examples abound. Margaret Mitchell's *Gone with the Wind*: 38 rejections. Anne Frank's *The Diary of a Young Girl* was rejected fifteen times. *Carrie* by Stephen King was rejected thirty times. *Zen and the Art of Motorcycle Maintenance* by Robert M. Pirsig amassed 121 denials. You get the idea.

The takeaway? First, remember this: no matter how noble or charitable you might be, you are the center of your world. Expect the same from others. To them, it's all about them—not you. That doesn't mean they aren't kind, giving, loving people. Just don't expect everyone to love you. Don't expect everyone to care who you are or what you do. And when they don't, don't take it personal and don't stop living your life and loving yourself, because, after all, it is *your* life. Stop worrying about whether or not someone wants the old coffee mugs you tossed into your free box. You had your use of them. You've exhausted your need. Let the emotion go.

"You probably wouldn't worry about what people think of you if
you could know how seldom they do."
~ Olin Miller

Today, focus on winning a battle.

Do you lean on *excuses* (such as New Year's Day) to make your resolution to quit smoking, lose weight, go back to school, or get a better job? Try this instead: Choose a random date as your springboard (today is good).

During November, December, and January we're bombarded with "special offers" for finding our soul mate, losing weight, and smoking cessation because marketers know that's when most of us make resolutions. But in so doing, we're also giving ourselves an *excuse* to put it off. "Come new year, no more chocolate ... tobacco ... TV ... More exercise. More reading. Naturally, you tell yourself that it's okay to go ape shit till then because, "Come January 1st ..."

On January 2nd or any date thereafter (until next January 1st, of course), you experience feelings of disappointment, sadness, or worthlessness if you lapse. How do you compensate for those feelings? You guessed it. Smoke. Eat. Stare at a TV.

Pick a day, say ... *today*, and follow your resolution for the day. See how it feels. Then tomorrow, stretch it a bit longer. Maybe a day and a half. Train yourself not to see short-term lapses as long-term failures and to recognize each short-term achievement as a success. For instance, if you typically smoke a pack of cigarettes a day, going without for three hours *is* a success. Remind yourself of the ones you *didn't* smoke during that time, not about the one you smoked during hour four. Get into the habit of catching yourself doing something *right*.

Give yourself permission to give yourself permission. Many will tell you that won't work. But I'm not selling you the clinic, the pre-packaged, delivered to your door, brightly labeled miracle elixirs, the smoke-free cigarettes, or the gym membership. I'm selling you on a great version of *you*. And that's both the easiest and hardest job. The best you is already here. Why not have it around a few years longer? Give yourself permission to live. But (yup ... here it comes), recognize that if you do nothing you'll achieve nothing. You'll also find that few things in life are fail-proof. The only way to fail-proof your life is to not live it.

You're on the clock. Start your day with the dedication and self-affirmation and build on yesterday. See just what you have inside yourself. You might just be amazed. And here's a little secret—it all begins upstairs. In your head. As Henry Ford said, "Whether you think you can, or you think you can't—you're right."

You don't have to win the war today. Focus on the battle. Using cigarettes as example; if you smoked twenty yesterday and nineteen today—you won a battle. You can't win a war without racking up some battle victories along the way. And you don't have to fight all of the battles at the same time. There will always be battles to fight. The flies, mosquitoes, bees, and wasps. You fight them one at a time. You set the limits.

Speaking of limits—have you learned yours? Have you drawn a line in the sand? I hope not. Because once you accept it, you'll never attempt crossing it. Limitations are like boxing rounds—small battles you fight to win the war. You learn from each round, take the lesson, adapt, and when the bell rings, you have another go at it. Each bell is an opportunity to fight anew and push perceived limits further away. You might not win every round, but if you accept that you will lose every one, you will. Keep punching.

Keep pushing. It's hard to beat someone who refuses to quit. Slow progress is still progress.

You climb your ladder one rung at a time. You win some, you lose some. It's "rock, paper, scissors" played out in real life. There's work involved. Get off your rear and do something. Anything. Go. Do. Win a battle today.

"Ninety-nine percent of all failures come from people who have a habit of making excuses."

~ George Washington Carver

It's like panning for gold.

"Even the best writer has to erase." This Spanish proverb is a personal favorite. No matter who you are, you've made (and will continue making) mistakes. Oodles of them. And when we make a mistake, we're faced with a choice. We either learn from it or we ignore it and keep banging our heads against the wall thinking, "Why me? How come bad things always happens to me?"

"Life finds a way," is another way of saying that sometimes life *gets in the way.* You won't always score the winning goal, get to make the final decision, or choose what happens next. As often as not, you won't. And yes, that sucks. The saying that the world doesn't owe you a living is true. Don't let your life get in the way of your life. *You* make your life. No one else. Not Mom. Not Dad. Not your brothers. Not your sisters. But life finds a way. Be open to it and (more importantly) ready for it. One way or another, life seems to continually find ways to surprise us. Staying present in your life makes it easier to face the waves when the waters rage.

Just when it seems you need a little encouragement, you're standing right there. If you depend on someone else to solve your problems, it's going be a long, bumpy journey. And your problems will he handled to the satisfaction of someone else—not you. At the end of the day, it's all you. You will make it what it becomes. Sometimes you'll get to play the hand you deal, sometimes you have to play the hand you're dealt. Sometimes you get a royal flush and other times the cards bite you square on the ass.

Bad things happen to everyone. Step one is to stop complaining about it. If you don't try to change it, you've no right to complain about it. Learn the lessons, and forge onward. Like writing *fasst* instead of fast, but erasing fasst only to write it as *faast*. Nothing is solved, but perhaps a lesson was learned. You have to keep plugging away, making determined effort, using new approaches. Your goal is to erase the mistake *once*, sweep the stubby eraser pieces off the page, pick up the pencil, and begin the next page of your life story. It's only a mistake if you don't act on it. If you act on it, it's a lesson. If you don't, it's your own doing.

Needing an eraser isn't a bad thing. The problem arises when you need it, have it, and don't use it. Setbacks are part of life. Common maladies we all push through at various times. But quitting at the first sign of a hurdle or struggle is like swimming to the middle of a deep river and then giving up because you have a cramp. Would you? No. You'd keep swimming, looking earnestly towards the safety of shore. To reach the safety, you have to swim the river and work through the pain. Sink or swim.

Many of us get frustrated and give up just before we achieve our breakthrough. We persevere to the tipping point then walk away. Like panning for gold, you have to keep at it, hunched over, sweat beads sliding with little splooshs into the stream. You shake that screen over and over and over, hoping, hunting, searching for a little tiny nugget that says "this is all worthwhile." Such is life.

"Once you learn to quit, it becomes a habit."
~ Vince Lombardi

I have the best job ever!

Do you recognize the differences between a Beethoven and Bach string quartet piece? If so, I'll bet you could also explain their divergent styles and nuances in a manner that musical neophytes could understand.

How would you describe yourself—a complex being—in a manner that others would understand? No fair using the usual "quiet, outgoing, fun, extroverted, shy, bookish" dating site lingo. Reach down and yank out your essence. The core of *you*. This can be a frightening (and powerful) exercise.

We devote substantial amounts of time acquiring education, skills, jobs, advancement, professional recognition, and pay. Why then, do so many invest such a comparatively trifling percentage in learning who they are as a person?

You are not defined by what you do. It is part of who you are, perhaps a large part. But at the end of the day, your salutation could easily be, "Hi, I'm (name) and I work at Earth as a human being. And I'm the only one of me there. It's a pretty cool gig!"

"Most people are other people. Their thoughts are someone else's opinions, their lives a mimicry, their passions a quotation."

~ Oscar Wilde

Whose photo is taped to your mirror?

Take away a person's enormous wealth or fame, strip them bare-ass naked then tell me how much they differ from anyone else. There's an Italian proverb attesting, "At the end of the game, the king and the pawn go back in the same box." Just as inevitable, this life will end for each of us, rich and poor alike.

Even so, we view others through our own filtered light; sifted and neatly sorted into cozy spaces. Some are gently placed on a pedestal. Some on a soap box. Others remain just a face in the crowd. But strip them down—the rich, powerful, famous, infamous, political, poor, and historical—you get just one thing: a naked human. Just sacks of fluids held together by bone and tendons and muscle. Beneath the make-up, inside the designer clothes, burrowed below the paint and lotions and sprays: Human Beings.

Even with these obvious facts, many wake each day to a photo of someone else taped to their mirror. Emulation? A crush? Desire? Infatuation? Admiration? Why wish to be someone other than who you already are? Why see someone else in a better light than you see yourself when there is but one of you? You shortchange yourself and your creator—what or whomever that or they may be. Take down the posters and put up more mirrors.

We look up to other people's accomplishments. To the attention they get for those accomplishments. Continually comparing ourselves to those posters taped on the walls and mirrors. It's human nature. Our parents did it to us. Our friends do it. Our partners do it. We do it to ourselves. It's the whole "Look what XYZ did!" Thus continues a cycle of trying to be like someone else simply to please someone else. You don't wish you were them. You wish other people saw you *as* them.

When you admire someone's accomplishments, use their example as your springboard. A baseline. Set your bar above, or aside from, what others have achieved. They are cooking life using their own recipe. You have the same ingredients. Some scarcer perhaps, others more abundant. You might use less or more of something or you might create something so off the wall that you can't help but be so original and unique as to have just raised the bar on everyone.

The only thing you should see when you look into your mirror is your reflection. It's the creators, the innovators, those that do as if it has never been done or do what's never been done or previously thought possible that you want staring back from your mirror. In other words—you.

"Behavior is the mirror in which everyone shows their image."
~ Johann Wolfgang von Goethe

The greatest thing since sliced bread.

Ever wonder why police officers often wear hats? In addition to providing protection from the elements, the hats serve as identification to other police personnel. When pursuing suspects, this helps reduce the chance that they will be accidentally wounded by friendly fire. The hats also enable civilians to more easily spot a police officer. We're taught from a young age to trust the police, and, as adults, most of us don't think twice about obeying the person waving us through a busy intersection or asking to see our identification. We're accustomed to associating the uniform, badge, and hat as signs of authority.

The uniform and accessories are for more than tradition and ease of identification though. Studies suggest that the uniforms psychologically influence how police personnel are publically perceived. For these reasons and others, the hats are sometimes referred to as *crowns of authority*. We see a uniform, badge, and hat—we think "law enforcement." The influence provided by those accouterments gives the wearer thought leadership; those who are among the first we think of in times of crises.

An easy way to visualize thought leadership is that it's the first person or organization that pops to mind on any given subject, product, or service. Examples include Volvo (safety), Google (Web search and innovation), or even Bic (affordable office pens and supplies).

It's worth noting that thought leadership applies to the downside as well. Few of us associate Enron with warm fuzzies, yet for many, they do hold thought leadership in a number of areas (i.e. accounting fraud and the subsequent "Enron scandal").

In our personal lives, we see thought leadership as *emotional leadership*. The person that comes to mind when you think of anger or love or narcissism or giving and so on through the emotional gamut. In your life, what image are you projecting? What image do you want to project? More importantly, are your actions in line with your self-perception? If not, you'll be labeled a phony. A counterfeit. Counterfeit people are like counterfeit money. It looks good and we want as much of it as we can get or hands on until we realize what it is.

Not everyone is going to think you're the greatest thing since sliced bread. But then, your goal shouldn't be to try and get everyone to adore you (if it is, good luck with that). You gain thought leadership just for being you. For being known as *that* person. Whomever you choose that person to be.

"Always remember—how you see yourself will be readily apparent to others."

~ Michael

The truth, the whole truth, and nothing but the truth.

Do you consider your beliefs to be absolute truths? Sure, some are. If you believe that 2 + 2 = 4, belief accurate. But we also have deep, personal beliefs that others might consider debatable, but we hold firm in their unassailability. Let's take a look at where beliefs come from and how they become so engrained that our brains process them as irrefutable facts.

Like folklore, some tales have been told so often that we believe they must be true. Or, we read about something from a respected authority or prominent institution and thus it must be cold, hard fact (the world is flat).

In our personal lives, we make stuff up and repeat it so often as to actually believe it to be true. Now, this does have potential benefit—the "fake it till you make it" approach to things. You tell yourself you can do something over and over until you believe yourself and take action. (*Note*: if you don't act on the belief, you really are just faking it.)

Beliefs influence how we feel, and thus, how we act or react in given circumstances. For better or worse, most of us had no choice but to listen to authority figures (parents, teachers) during our formative years. If you could break free from all the beliefs that have been accumulated since childhood—especially the negatives (you will never, you can't possibly, don't even consider ...)—and rebuild your belief system what would it look like? What would it encompass? (Hopefully a lot of, "I will, I can, I'm going to.")

You'll never have life completely figured out. And if you think you do—send a postcard and let everyone know how it's going in the land of unicorns and tooth fairies. In return, I'll send you one from, "I'm figuring this stuff out as I go along." Because that's where most of us are on a daily basis.

Your belief system will probably be an amalgam of parental tenets, school disciplines, and a coachload of life observations and experiences. Center your beliefs on your desires and follow your inner voice. My 2 + 2 will equal 4; same as you. But, your 2 + 2 is uniquely yours.

"*Your beliefs become your thoughts, your thoughts become your words, your words become your actions, your actions become your habits, your habits become your values, your values become your destiny.*"

~ Mahatma Gandhi

Look back, but live forward.

There are those who say they don't have a lot to look forward to in life and use that excuse to erode themselves and ooze into decline until they fit perfectly into their pre-imagined coffin.

Funny, when the same people win the lotto they start exercising, eating healthy, and taking care of themselves because then they want to live forever and enjoy all that money can buy. You know, many of the experiences they could have enjoyed *without* money.

Would you agree to shave a year off your life for fifty dollars? How about five-hundred dollars? A thousand? Of course not. It ain't the money. Money was an excuse. We all *say* it's the money till we have it and we're still miserable. Many people are poor because the only thing they have is money. It's then that they realize money is, at best, a numbing agent. A game of "my pile is bigger than your pile." (Want to win or end that game without playing? Easy. Just say, "Congratulations. I'm happy for you." And mean it. Game over. You win.)

Don't let the things you want make you forget what you already have. Keep pushing, keep striving, keep moving towards your best you, but don't overlook all that you accomplished to get where you are. Greek philosopher Epicurus said it succinctly, "Do not spoil what you have by desiring what you have not; remember that what you now have was once among the things you only hoped for."

You can look back. Just don't live back there. Use that rear wall as support, but keep your eyes ahead, focused on your future. Former first lady (and amazing individual in her own right), Eleanor Roosevelt, had some wise words about this, stating, "I am who I am today because of the choices I made yesterday." Our yesterdays are learning tools. They provide our internal radar and enable us to benefit from a lifetime of smell, touch, taste, sight, love found and love lost, joy, and agony. We fill our toolboxes with yesterdays and use them today to build our tomorrows.

"Learn from yesterday, live for today, hope for tomorrow. The important thing is to not stop questioning."

~ Albert Einstein

I'll hold the ladder for you.

Low-hanging fruit. In business, it's a common metaphor for doing easy tasks first—tasks easiest to complete, goals easiest to achieve, problems easiest to solve. Many choose to end their harvest after picking only the low-hanging fruit, when actually that's just the onset of the potential harvest.

One of the easy excuses associated with picking life's low-hanging fruit is an illusion of immediate, long-term success; that once harvested, everything is complete. Realistically, low-hanging fruit is what you reach before embarking on the real work— climbing your life ladder. And that ascension will require a bit more effort than picking a shoulder-high apple from a dangling tree branch. There'll be some strolling, some running, some stretching, and some leaping. You'll even manage a respite or two.

You'll quickly find that the playing field doesn't begin level and everyone's ladder doesn't have the same number of rungs. Financially, some have access to more low-hanging fruit than others. But we all have our own ladder to climb and we all seek our own purpose, including those born with the proverbial silver spoon in their mouth. Perhaps Mommy and Daddy's trust fund is their low-hanging fruit and will serve as a tool that helps create great things. At the end of the day though, someone can give you land, lumber, fixtures, tools, and cash, but you still have to design and build your home. (Not *a* house. *Your home.*)

There's only so much low-hanging fruit, and once it's picked, you're going to have to climb to reach the really good stuff. Onward and upward and sometimes leaning off the ladder sideways. In its literal use, picking only "low-hanging fruit" allows the majority to over-ripen, and to eventually fall from the tree; leaving only bushels of squishy, odorous, rotten fruit. Fruit wasted. Fruit meant for you to savor.

Grab the easy pickins', then climb your ladder. There's much waiting to be discovered. Adventures you simply can't experience standing around doing nothing, waiting for someone else's leftovers to fall at your feet.

" *You can't stay in your corner of the forest waiting for others to come to you. You have to go to them sometimes.*"

~ A.A. Milne

You know, space and stuff.

I'd just finished cleaning up the kitchen after a casual dinner party when a friend looked around and commented on how clean and crisp everything was. She said she liked the minimalist approach, wanted to try it, but couldn't figure out what to do with all her stuff. I told her that she'd just solved her quandary by recognizing that it's just "stuff."

I shared the opinion that even if you have 10,000 square feet of space, it doesn't mean you have to fill 10,000 sq. ft. of space with *stuff*. It's possible to fill space with nearly nothing physical as long as the space itself is personally meaningful. You can walk into a 100 sq. ft. room and be totally moved or overwhelmed and enter a 10,000 sq. ft. space and be completely bored. Whether a space is physically empty or full, it is also mentally empty or full.

Most of us tend to think we need all the money we have and all the space we own or rent (plus that storage locker filled with more stuff)—all the while using only the portion of the brain needed to gain the space, money, and "stuff." Making a house a home is more placing photos on the walls. It's the walls that do the talking. It's not the size of the room, it's the size of your mind that matters most.

"That's all you need in life, a little place for your stuff. That's all your house is: a place to keep your stuff. If you didn't have so much stuff, you wouldn't need a house. You could just walk around all the time."

~ George Carlin

It's a bird, it's a plane. It's you!

"She is a professional singer." Okay, makes sense; she sings for a living. "No, wait. She's *famous*." Okay, got it. "No, you don't understand. She's a *star*." Okay. Got it. "No, no, no. You aren't listening—she is a *superstar*!"

When did we start placing humans on the same level as things astrophysicists are exploring throughout the cosmos? And what is the implication to us bourgeois "regular folk?"

It's a myth of perfection. Something that helps us escape from our day to day living through photoshopped models, a surgically rendered dimple or two, and a spin doctor massage, all leading to an artificial reality loaded with envy. And, in the event you are "perfect" in every way? You're not. We are all broken in some fashion or another. We all have our fears and concerns—whether an illness, missing an appointment, or chipping a nail.

Use the reflection of the mirror in your soul as well as the one on the wall. Be true to yourself. Don't set yourself up for failure by grasping at something that doesn't even exist. None of us is perfect. Nada. Get over yourself to get on with yourself. Ignore the myth of perfection. At the end of the day strive to be the best "you" that you can be. Be a "Super *you*!"

"Have no fear of perfection - you'll never reach it."
~ Salvador Dali

It's not the losing, it's the quitting that creates failure.

Sometimes timing really is everything. I'd spent all day one rainy Saturday painting the master bathroom. Sanding, taping, spackling, priming, bending, stooping, reaching, wedging the step ladder into corners, nearly kissing the back of the toilet trying to paint along the baseboard. Ugh. About nine hours later, I'd finally finished.

I'd chewed off a big chunk of the clean-up process and was still in my painting clothes (or should I say, *painted* clothes), when the doorbell rang. I answered, brush in hand. It was a young college student going around the neighborhood offering his painting services. He looked at me. At my clothing. At the paint brush. Before I could say anything, he smiled, muttered "crap," gave a ballet-worthy spin and walked away. I couldn't help but chuckle. Who hasn't missed out on an opportunity by just *that much*?

I noted though that it was only a momentary discouragement, as he continued his trek through the neighborhood—knocking on doors and handing out flyers. I may have just finished, but perhaps the person behind the next door he knocks on is only beginning. He was finding rejection, but not quitting. That's a smart path to success.

"*The spirit, the will to win, and the will to excel are the things that endure. These qualities are so much more important than the events that occur.*"

~ Vince Lombardi

Speaking of never giving up ...

I have a friend who was experiencing an irregular heartbeat. After a battery of tests and the obligatory (and wise) second opinion, it was determined that a pacemaker was the best long-term treatment option.

My friend's doctor told him that a primary benefit is that if his heartbeat dropped below 35 beats per minute, the pacemaker would start automatically. His big concern? That when it was his time to leave this world, the pacemaker would keep kicking in just as he was getting comfortable. Not, "Oh, Lord, I'm going to die," not, "What if the battery malfunctions?" He did not have those worries. Only the acknowledgement that the time comes for all of us, and when it's time, it's time.

Now, he's also in no rush to leave this life and did have the pacemaker installed. I can't help but smile and applaud his outlook on life. We could all learn from pacemakers. When struggles appear unsurmountable, use your life tools and experiences, kick into overdrive, and keep on pumping. (And my friend is doing just that!)

"I urge all of you, all of you, to enjoy your life, the precious moments you have. To spend each day with some laughter and some thought, to get your emotions going."

~ Jim Valvano

Stereotypes are convenient boxes.

Everyone has someone in their life that isn't quite right in their head. Is it you? Being the odd one doesn't make you weird. Different? Maybe. Bad? Nope. None of us is precisely like anyone else. Maybe others aren't right in the head. Or maybe, most plausible, *none* of us is right in the head based on the usual definition of "normal" (*conforming to the standard or the common type; regular*). You get to define your normal. If people think you're quirky, just smile and relish having the courage to be you. Celebrate those things that make you unique and respect that others enjoy the same individuality in their lives. Avoid the easy tendency to measure others by your expectations and desires.

If you like country music, is someone lesser to you because they enjoy jazz? Some instances may be obvious because stereotypes are often held to be absolute truths (e.g. a person from Alabama who loves country music must hate hip hop.) But that is a stereotype. A fundamental issue with legends, lore, or stereotyping is that even when established on a strand of truth, they perpetuate and grow over time with lessening validation required for it to be "true."

As example, let's say a small town has four residents pass away over a two week period, all age 71, all having owned green cars at the time of their passing. It makes its way around the coffee shops, schools, and so on, until it becomes "fact" that owning a green car means you're going to die at age 71. Well, a few years go by and low and behold, a 71 year old passes away and amazingly—they owned a green car. The legend grows, is validated, and again solidifies itself as a "truth." Naturally, anytime something occurs that does not support that "truth," reasons are found to invalidate not the perceived truth but the anomaly. (We all want to be right.)

Only when you open your eyes, ears, and mind will you truly make decisions based on your individual truths. Not everyone will agree with your opinions. But, disagreement, discussion, and debate are great learning sources. Besides, if two people agree on everything—one of them is unnecessary.

" The only person you are destined to become is the person you decide to be."

~ Ralph Waldo Emerson

Focus, focus, focus.

Information overload. Infobesity. Drinking from a fire hydrant. Whatever you call it, there is more information available than ever (and growing by the moment). With the plethora of material out there, finding what we're looking for should be easier, not harder. Indeed, it isn't an information glut that creates the roadblock. It's the information consumer. The inability or unwillingness to doggedly focus on a desired outcome.

In our business lives we use productivity tools. We flag emails, add keywords, set up junk boxes, use time management tools, etc. Like going on a weight loss program though, one of the most effective tools available—at no cost—is *discipline*. The staunch determination to stay focused and committed to the goal at hand. Our short attention spans, coupled with a natural curiosity (a great thing), and no self-imposed deadline do us in.

Example: Let's say you have space for a small garden and spring is right around the corner. You're interested but not sure where to begin. You Google "small garden." Right away, you find images for small gardens. So you poke around in the photos, getting ideas. You find one you like, thinking, "oh, that one's cute," and you click the link. It leads to a blog about someone tired of the smog and auto exhaust ruining her tomatoes. After five or so minutes of commiserative reading and silent nodding of agreement, you return to your search results. Wait—what's this? An article about small garden design ideas. Better check it out. "Using a sawzall to clear laurel bushes and small tree limbs." Fascinating. Wait. What's a sawzall? Google.

Now you're browsing a home improvement warehouse site, doing a sub-search on sawzalls. Wait! Cordless screwdrivers. You think, "That's what I need to hang those curtains. I thought my wrist was going to go numb from all those fasteners." You read on devouring the information. Affordable, good battery life (But no spare), padded rubber grip. You decide to keep looking. Here's one with a spare battery included. Nice. Pricier, but seems like a good deal. I better check the reviews. Huuum. This guy says not to bother with a cordless screwdriver and just get a decent rechargeable drill because it can be used for a lot more than just screws. Good call. But pricier yet. You wonder, "Will I use it enough to offset the cost?" Google.

You key in, "Why do I need a rechargeable drill?" and hit enter. Wow, those are some interesting stories. And the funny ones are a crack up. I'm going to forward the one about the woman that drilled into a PVC pipe and sprouted a kitchen water leak to my friend, Lisa. She'll think it's a hoot! What is a PVC pipe, anyway? Google.

"PVC pipe." Well, come to find, PVC pipe has oodles of uses. Some larger gardens use PVC pipe for irrigation. "Well," you think aloud, "Great idea! I should look into planting a small garden right here at home!" You decide that after lunch you'll check into gardening ideas that would fit the size of your yard.

Like life, it's discovering as you go, learning what to look for, what to let pass, and what to tuck away for later. The key is to pinpoint the problem, focus on the information that provides a solution, and follow-through with appropriate action. Of course, searching for and identifying solutions was both easier and more difficult before today's glut of available information. I heard someone once say that it's possible to reach the end of the Internet. I doubt that's true. I better research it. *Google.*

If your challenge is determining what type of paint to use on a bedroom wall; worry about fall jacket styles another time.

"I'm facing Niagara Falls—the wind and the mist and the dark and the peregrine falcons—and I'm going to stay focused on the other side."

~ Nik Wallenda

Life's a Beet, Then You Die.

I don't like beets. I didn't like them as a kid, don't like them as an adult. I do not enjoy cold soup. The saying goes, "*Revenge* is a dish best served cold." Revenge. *Not* soup. So in my mind, it stands to reason that beets and cold soup should not be used as a mash-up to create anything that might accidently get near my mouth.

So along comes the cold variety of borscht. Oh sure, borscht can be made without beets, such as the tomato paste-based "orange borscht," but I'm still not buying it. It contains a whole bunch of ingredients that my mother dutifully tried washing out of my bib many times in those days of developing taste buds.

I advocate that trying new and different things makes life adventurous. That variety and discovery is what makes life enjoyable and exciting. So, I decided it was time to eat my own words as it were. I took the approach that by sitting at a restaurant table and ordering borscht, I was experiencing life outside my comfort zone. Something new. A culinary adventure for the timid (me!). I fidgeted, made small talk, and looked longingly at the "real" food being delivered to surrounding tables. Then my moment of truth. The borscht arrived. Quicker than any restaurant appetizer I'd ever ordered in my life.

I tucked in, placed the spoon between my thumb, index, and middle finger (you just looked at your hand, didn't you), and scooped up my first mini-ladle of borscht. I did it! And I discovered something.

I don't like beets. I didn't like them as a kid, don't like them as an adult. I do not enjoy cold soup. But now I can say it with self-acquired knowledge and authority, and put the experience in the memory folder, filed under "Nope!"

But, I did learn a few things. By climbing over my usual walls and into uncharted territory, I gained a tad bit of confidence, a dollop of accomplishment, and removed another brick from the wall that would otherwise separate me from meeting life challenges head-on.

It's all part of the adventure.

"Meriwether Lewis and William Clark forged the trail. The rest of us are followers; commuters fighting for a parking space."

~ Michael

Today is your lucky day.

Today you have the opportunity to make choices that affect not only today, but the rest of your life. You begin each day with a clean slate. Then again, that makes *every* day your lucky day. And everything you do today adds another building block to your tomorrow.

Every little bit makes a difference. Everything. Consider: the average step length (according to the University of Oklahoma Health Sciences Center), is approximately twenty-six inches for women and thirty-one inches for men. For example sake, let's use an average stride of twenty-eight inches. If you walk for just *sixty seconds* a day—sixty small steps; in one year you'll have covered over 9.67 miles (15.56 km).

Make it a point to do at least one small thing every day that brings you closer to your goals. Keep a journal. You will be surprised how much you accomplish by breaking it down into baby steps. Don't waste time lamenting what you believe you can't do, tackle what you *can* do. Over time, you'll find your "can't do" list shrinking and your *"am doing"* list growing. It all starts upstairs— in your head. Success begets success.

"It's not that you have to make a decision; but that you get to make a choice."

~ Michael

Change is Coming!

So far, we've looked a bit inwards at ourselves and talked about life itself and provided some tools to help guide the way.

Now, we're going to muddy the waters for a while by adding other people into the mix. Yup. We're going to discuss dealing with other people and relationships. Don't worry, it won't hurt a bit, and you'll come through this section with flying colors.

Onward!

"You don't develop courage by being happy in your relationships everyday. You develop it by surviving difficult times and challenging adversity."

Epicurus

It's complicated.

Love. A small word. An enormous word. A word with as many definitions as there are people. A word personal and unique to each of us. Love. A most beautiful, most precious thing. Unfortunately it can also be the most painful. There's always a catch.

We love our brothers, sisters, parents, and friends. And we believe that we are *in* love with our significant other. But how do you define being in love? Is it the, "oh my goodness, he's the one, I can just tell!"? Or is that just the beginning? What happens when infatuation and newness wane, when the holes in your life that another person fills slowly fade into the background? That's when the work begins. Maintaining, nurturing, and feeding love. Or risk "in love" fading to simple love, which, in turn, fades to "I care," and on down the slippery slide to *indifference*. Don't let anyone kid you; it's work keeping the "in" in love.

How will you know when you've found love? How do you define the emotion? Why do some people trash good relationships in the hopes of finding more of the same elsewhere? Some people spend copious amounts of time thinking about, striving-praying-hoping for, a magical "it." You ask yourself, "How will I know for certain?" Is it that initial burst of excitement, the butterflies-in-your-tummy feeling that happens just at the mere sound of a voice? We know those euphoric feelings won't last forever. So then you might find yourself wondering, "When those feelings end, am I *out* of love?"

If you're not out of love, then where did that epic, sweaty, longing, pin wheeling feeling go? Have you quit putting in the effort (make no mistake, there is much effort involved) to keep the relationship energy positive? Or is love a bit like many other parts of life and just relaxes into a nice, comfortable place to be? (I believe dentists and Pink Floyd refer to this as "comfortably numb.") A place that—while secure and safe—is no longer supplying the feelings you became addicted to? Does love grow with age and change with maturity much the same as we do as humans? Should it always leave us wanting more? In a perfect world we would find our soul mate, fall hopelessly in love, knowing with absolute certainty that they are the ordained complement to our life. Ah, for a perfect world.

If you didn't have the benefit of such an ideal scenario, you might find yourself meandering on an undefined path, looking to repeat that feeling anew. Of course, it's not to be found because the way in which you give and receive love has now been permanently altered.

Even if you were to stumble upon that mythical perfect partner, you'll still face hurdles. Once you tasted that initial spark you morphed into a different person. To be open to loving again, you must recalibrate your previous notion of how love would feel. The idea of a soul mate coming to rescue you from a hum-drum life makes for great theater, but doubtful reality at best. Besides you shouldn't be deprived of (or rescued from) life and its invaluable lessons.

An enduring relationship isn't just one where people love each other. It's one where two people continually seek affirming ways to love each another. Too many people pick apart their love by trying to categorize it or by frequently questioning themselves: "Am I in love?"

Do the bells and whistles chime and squeal forever? Probably no longer than a new car smell. As with the auto, we like it, enjoy it, embrace it, and life goes rolling along. If those initial feelings did last, I think it would eventually kill us. I doubt our bodies are equipped to handle so much adrenaline for extended periods. At minimum, we'd burn out on the thought of being in love, as the burden of always being overwhelmed and out-of-control would be a weight too great to carry.

That said, it *is* imperative to continually stoke the romantic fire. All those little gestures add up. Consider nine seconds. That's a minute amount of time and really all it takes to demonstrate to someone their importance in your life. You don't have to move mountains or make the earth quake beneath their feet. Love, attention, affection, respect ... nine seconds at a time. Not ten. Nine. Easy to remember, and just as easy to put in to action. Consider—if you do just three small, loving things a day, that's only twenty-seven seconds. Fewer than three hours a year. No downside, huge upside. Here's an example for you: "I love you, don't forget to turn off the coffee maker, and the car is out of gas!" is not one sentence. Three *unrelated* sentences.

Take a few seconds and catch someone doing something right. Or as hall of fame collegiate basketball coach and Presidential Medal of Freedom recipient John Wooden stated, "It's the little details that are vital. Little things make big things happen." Love isn't always as obvious in its grandeur as many want to believe.

Even in (especially in) the longest of relationships, there are still moments, glints as they may be, that you'll "feel it" all over again. You'll espy your partner and the butterflies take root. Everything old is new. A recipe for an enduring loving relationship contains a few, simple key ingredients:

- Respect your partner as they too struggle through this thing called life.
- "Home" is a person, not a place.
- When you need a soft place to fall, you know they'll do their best to catch you.

Lasting loves are reciprocating and are flexible during fluid life challenges, respect individual growth, and remain supportive and protective; bending without breaking. Independent growth enhances the relationship. In this case, two cooks in the kitchen are totally acceptable.

Sometimes it's not enough just having that person *in* your life, but rather showing them how incredibly important they are *to* your life. Simple, right? But friends get in the way. Work gets in the way. Life gets in the way. Yes, we all have to work, earn, and serve a worldly purpose. But your partner should never have to guess whether they are a primary spark in your life's engine. Always possible? Nope. But a fine aspiration. For those currently in a relationship, appreciate the fact that you have someone who loves you and work each day to love them more, instead of looking for easy reasons to love them less.

In life, we experience numerous hurdles, obstacles, and adventures. When you have someone to love, and who loves you back, the more time in your life you have to grow in that love and together face those hurdles, meet challenges, and cherish the adventure—hand in hand. Two heads are better than one, and two hearts can be divided by none.

Over the years, I've interviewed dozens of people and couples: those in newer relationships, seasoned relationships, and those freshly in and out of relationships. I believe that there's no cupid's arrow that will magically *sustain* a loving relationship. And while (depending on your personal belief) there was or wasn't a Garden of Eden, most of us want to believe in the concept of that place where life is good, someone loves you and you them, the sky is always blue, birds are always singing, there is a babbling brook, and life just goes as you want it and have always dreamed about. As long as you are dreaming, do your part to make it a reality.

Caring for significant relationships requires substantial work and effort. We get engulfed by life's demands and don't see the forest for the trees. "Where's my tie, are the kids ready, did you gas up the car, I just spilled coffee all over my blouse, the lawn needs mowing, you need to help my brother move this weekend." What happened to the big picture?

At the end of the day your job is not your life. Your life is your job. Some find that easier to accept than others, but most all of us do ... eventually. Unfortunately, like a slowly-eroding cliff or riverbank, many don't see it till it's too late. Too many avoid discovering the secret of loving success because deep down they suspect the secret may be hard work. It is. Just break it down to small, meaningful actions. Cruise ships can't turn on a dime. It takes time. Relationships are much the same way. You get headed in a dangerous direction, you can't fix it overnight. When people begin seeing life *through* or *past* their partner instead of with them, it's time to slow the ship and begin the turn to calmer seas. You have the helm, you control the rudder.

In the end, living a loving life is really one of the most important things we can do. But we sure can make it complicated though, can't we?

"If the house were on fire, what is the one thing you'd rescue?"

And he replied, "You."

~ Michael

We get smarter every day.

Each of us is a unique product of our individual wiring, interests, background, education, DNA, and surroundings. But when it comes to relationships, it's usually common denominators that bring people together (so claim bazillions of dating sites). Merging those commonalities with individual and diverse interests helps cement the unique relationship bond—even as you continue growing (emotionally and intellectually) as an individual.

Outside interests strengthen your social network and sense of personal identity, and brings new insights and stimulation to your partnership. Fresh perspectives and new topics for conversation.

Thinking your relationship is "fine just the way it is," leaves no room for flexibility or growth—both key ingredients to a mutually satisfying partnership. Trying to maintain a status quo is a bit like having a desert landscape in the middle of a rain forest. Even if you can accomplish it, and both your partner and you want the sand, chances are, at some point one of you will yearn for rain. This means you will eventually have to talk about it or risk the tidal wave of resentment that will follow in its wake.

"I wanted to move to Seattle, but she wouldn't discuss it. I wound up baking in this forsaken desert like a suburban nomad all this time." Oh-oh. The consequences of not having the conversation are about to come home to roost. There will be the inevitable "he-said, she-said" and the "you should have said," and "how come you didn't." Through it all, there has to be simple recognition that life is fluid and nothing or no one will remain as they are in their present form (oh, how boring).

Trying to morph into someone you aren't simply to appease someone or gain their affection is not a sustainable or desirable endeavor. When it's all said and done, you can't point a finger at your partner and hold them responsible for your disappointments. Take personal responsibility, take time for yourself, follow your dreams, and share it all within a supportive, nurturing relationship. Blaming another for not getting what you want out of your life only erodes your relationship's foundation. You can only truly change yourself.

"It's easier to get along when neither person expects the other to be perfect."

~ Michael

Touchdown!

Healthy relationships are an important part of a vibrant life. No news flash there. But I imagine there are as many definitions of "healthy" as there are relationships, and what works for some will not work for others. Stands to reason that before you can build and sustain a healthy relationship, you need to identify what one looks like *to you*.

Don't ignore or overlook those things that are potential sources of future frustration. Things you might presently brush off for fear of derailing what you hope will flourish into a lasting relationship. Keep in mind though, if something irritates you now, it'll likely irritate you later. Don't go into a relationship with a goal of moulding someone to your personal specifications. It's better to just have those hard conversations early (yes, even though you "know its love").

I'm not suggesting you ask someone on your first date how many kids the two of you should have (mental image of person spewing their beverage across the room), but have an idea of what's important, what's *really* important, and then listen. If you want four children and he doesn't want any—thinking that "he'll come around" is like betting on that 100,000 to 1 long shot. It might happen, but don't quit your job until the check clears. Over time, if he continues reiterating his desire to not have children, take a moment and ask yourself: Should you be upset with him for not changing, or at yourself for not listening?

If he says he's a h-u-g-e football fan, your mind might believe it to mean, "oh, that's nice," but in reality he was telling you: he's a h-u-g-e American football fan. Face paint, chest tattoos, beer keg in the living room every Friday, Saturday, Sunday, and Monday August through February, sofa cushions full of cheese puffs, never misses a high school, college, pro, Canadian league, semi-pro, neighborhood pick-up game ... You get the idea. A stereotypical example, but easily imagined. It's easy to overlook or ignore things that seem trivial early that might drive you bonkers later. Later is too late. Ask the questions early. "What does being a h-u-g-e football fan mean anyway?"

"The game of life is a lot like football. You have to tackle your problems, block your fears, and score your points when you get the opportunity."
~ Lewis Grizzard

Pride goeth before a fall.

"Sometimes I think the best things when there's nobody there." Another for the "would have, could have, should have" slush pile. We think of the things we should have said and done, but didn't, lying in bed unable to sleep, staring at the ceiling. Mind in overdrive.

Sure, we have things that we should never compromise on, but sometimes we act out of stubbornness or just believing that we *have* to be right. Sometimes over really, really inane things. You wanted red wine, he wanted white. An argument ensues, one of you gets up and leaves in a huff. Foolish pride. Is that worth dinging the relationship?

Don't wait until it's too late. If you stop trying, they'll stop knocking. Don't wait till there is nobody there. Too many of us don't say "I love you" or "I need you" or "I'm sorry" because we don't hear it first.

Try this: Treat your partner the way you'd want your son or daughter treated. Seems simple enough, but we often don't follow this little tidbit of wisdom. We argue, yell, and fight about all kinds of trivial, menial stuff, but would never allow someone else to do that to our children. There's the lesson. End of blurb.

"Some people spend more time, energy, and effort parallel parking than on important relationships. Don't be them."

~ Michael

The St. Valentine's Day Dilemma

Valentine's Day (or the "Hallmark Holiday" as cynics often label it), rolls up on us every year. That day those in a relationship pretend to care for a person more than they did on February 13th or will on February 15th.

Some believe Valentine's Day is the opportunity to show they care (to which I'd counter that it's *an* opportunity, not *the* opportunity), while many detractors view February 14th as twenty-four hours loaded with obligations and duties. A chore rather than an opportunity. Still others see the day as having been hijacked by opportunistic businesses looking to make a quick buck, capitalizing on the "If you love me you would have, could have, should have ..." fever of the moment. A day with a built-in checklist where if one item is missed, serious consequences occur. "Lemme see ... Card? Check. Flowers? Check. The 'for no reason' phone call? Check." Lord help you if you miss something, or worse, fall short of what others may lavish on their partner. Damned if you do, damned if you don't.

Remember, Valentine's Day isn't a "get out of jail free" card. It's not a box of grocery store candy, a "must buy something shiny," or a BuyFlowersOrDie.com experience. How do you feel about that person the rest of the year? You still love and care for them, right? Why not demonstrate that appreciation and love every day—all year long? Do you need a calendar (or a greeting card company) to remind you to show gratitude and thankfulness? Does it take a big red heart circling a single day to prompt an expression of love from you?

Consider: Christians commonly celebrate the birth of Christ on December 25th, but continue to pray throughout the year, attending and participating in organized services and otherwise giving special thanks for the wonderful things in life. For Christians, December 25th is a *symbol* of something celebrated throughout the year. As is Valentine's Day.

So go ahead, celebrate the day. Just remember to celebrate the rest of the year as well. See, it isn't February 14th that's special. It's what February 14th *signifies* that's special. The other 364 days are just as singular.

"I don't understand why Cupid was chosen to represent Valentine's Day. When I think about romance, the last thing on my mind is a short, chubby toddler coming at me with a weapon."

~ Unknown

Speaking of …

Special dates of significance provide picture-perfect opportunities to reach out to friends, family, and other loved ones. But, if you wait *only* for anniversaries, holidays, birthdays, or other milestones, you'll be overlooking 99% of a year's opportunities to celebrate. If it's worth doing, do it. Follow your heart, not the calendar.

On a related note, even if we don't admit it, many of us experience more emotion (disappointment) from *not* getting a birthday gift than we do joy from receiving birthday recognition. For the giver, it has become an expectation: "Oh crap, I need to get this card in the mail right away." For the receiver, it's often simply a feeling of acknowledgement that the sender's e-calendar works. But forget that special day and *all bets are off*.

Want to stand out from the crowd? Send a random card. Create your own holiday. Send a certificate from your (self-invented) school. Know someone that loves gardening? Send them a degree from <your name> University bestowing honors for having successfully completed the required program of dirty hands, worn out jeans, trampled kitchen mud, and creator of the best damn fruit and veggie pantry on earth. Then you aren't one of many "expected" givers. You've got their full attention.

"It's said putting lipstick on a pig doesn't change anything. But I don't think anyone asked the boar."

~ Michael

Yes, more work.

A curious anomaly of marriage is that many people treat their marriage certificate like an extended warranty. They think once they're married that that piece of paper assures everything will be all right. No maintenance required. "Now that I have this, I can do anything I want. It's insured!" Like those rental cars we drive with much less care than we do our own—especially if we purchase the optional piece of paper (insurance).

Here's my prediction: Marriage certificate or not, if you don't perform regular maintenance and treat the relationship with love and respect, it will run poorly or most likely fail. Repairs aren't cheap and you won't like the policy's deductible either (you might have life insurance too, but you probably don't want to see if the policy pays off).

The grass is always greener ~~on the other side of the fence~~ when it's watered, fed, trimmed, and maintained.

The sooner you ...

- Say "you're sorry"
- Learn to forgive
- Show someone you love them
- Need them
- Want them in your life
- Succumb to your own happiness
- Learn to say "no"

... the sooner you'll discover life opening up to you, and the sooner you'll experience its power and freedom. Say it sooner. Do it sooner. Live now.

This revolves around taking personal responsibility and not expecting a committed relationship to come with a guarantee. The only guarantee is that relationships—all successful relationships—require active participation by both parties. Some people believe that if they feel badly about something long enough, someone will have to do something about it. Well, someone does. And they are that someone.

Playing the role of victim and expecting the world to jump at the chance to make things perfect for you is silly. You'll be miserable and the world won't care. No one else can (or should be given permission to) live your life for you or solve challenges in your stead. You'll create just as many troubles trying to avoid them or waiting for someone else to solve them than by facing them head on and getting on with life. It's okay to be upset if it rains on your parade but don't get all huffy if no one leaps up to hold an umbrella over your head.

"If you could kick the person in the pants responsible for most of your trouble, you wouldn't sit for a month."

~ Theodore Roosevelt

Zero–Based Affection.

I coined this phrase as the relationship equivalent of zero-based budgeting. In finance, zero-based budgeting is a scenario where every item of a budget must be evaluated before approval. Not just the changes. Thus, beginning from a zero-base. Our life relationships are built much the same way. We begin without concept of like or dislike, love or indifference. We see the other person with zero-based affection. The one time there is an empty slate that provides you with the opportunity to create the relationship you desire.

This is important because—as you know—relationships are loaded with barter and compromise. We work, tinker, beg, cajole, desire, and grab within them. Some seek counseling in times of need or crisis. Some choose to distance themselves, while still others pretend everything is just peachy, thank you. But you only get zero-based affection once. It can be used to create a night, a weekend, or a life. To paraphrase an old saying: You only get one chance to make your first impression. After that—everything has a history, a memory, and a life of its own. After zero, you work to balance your relationship assets and debits as best you can.

"You only get one opportunity to notice a new haircut."

~ Michael

Okay, love is complicated.

Duh. Now that we have that out of the way ...

Let's look at something you can do to make the path to love a little easier. Namely—learning to avoid a journey with someone that isn't going to pull their own weight. Someone not emotionally present.

There is no need to compound the already stressful challenges of dating by becoming involved with someone not who is not emotionally available. If you are looking for a committed relationship, choose consciously (yeah, yeah ... it was love at first sight. Then what?) Your life is too precious to squander time on a relationship that doesn't stand a chance from the get go. You deserve a partner who is emotionally available and is also looking to create and maintain a loving connection over time. It takes two.

Being emotionally *unavailable* refers to those who create barriers between themselves and others to (either consciously or subconsciously) avoid emotional intimacy.

Emotionally unavailable people are often depressing and distressing, and their partners feel neglected, unloved, and unwanted. Emotionally unavailable people will seek out relationships but the problems begin when they are unable, or unwilling, to commit. They do, however, frequently behave as if they want to be in a relationship, so it's important to recognize the signs. Here are some common signs:

- Emotionally unavailable people are difficult to nail down. Call them and get voice mail. Leave a message, and then wait forever for a return call—or they don't call at all.

- Emotionally unavailable people are unwilling to make plans or state their availability. And if they do make plans, they may forget and leave you hanging. No relationship is perfect, and even emotionally available people have jobs and obligations that interfere with their time with loved ones. In healthy relationships, people aren't joined at the hip and enjoy some autonomy. The difference is emotionally available people make time and make themselves available to the people important in their lives.

Bottom line: Determine if the person is as interested in a relationship as you. If so, are they interested in a relationship *with you*? If they are, you still must determine if that person is physically and mentally *available*.

~ *"Never spend time with people who don't respect you or consider you just an option."* ~

Is there a masterpiece in your life?

I was traipsing through the dining room heading for the kitchen when I saw something out of the corner my eye. It was a piece of raku pottery, sitting on the fireplace hearth between two elongated gothic-style candleholders. I stopped and picked it up, admiring the craftsmanship, color, detail, and finish. A beautiful piece. Later that afternoon I asked my other half about it. She replied that it was a gift from long ago and had been sitting on the hearth for years. Huh. I did a double-take. Huh. I'd been walking past this beautiful piece for years, less than two feet from me as I brushed back and forth in and out of the kitchen. Hundreds, if not thousands of times. Even so, I'd have been willing to bet that I'd never seen it before.

Unfortunately, that's often the way it becomes with people in our lives. It begins with passing admiration, escalates to desire, moves to having them as a large part of your life and cherishing them, then—if you aren't attentive and appreciative—deteriorates into taking them for granted, assuming they will always be there.

Do you have something or someone in your life that you've allowed to become transparent? If you own an original Picasso but seldom notice it, perhaps it'd be better appreciated in another environment. If you enjoy it, make time to see it for the first time all over again. And if the *what* is a *who*, take the time and show your appreciation and let them know the importance they hold in your life. After all, you only get so many opportunities at a Picasso.

If you allow that special person to become transparent you might one day be brought back to reality with a wake-up call like this:

"Maybe one day I'll be what you want. But don't wait too long, because the day you want me, may be the day I've finally given up."

Don't wait for things to get to that point before deciding to integrate (or re-integrate) yourself into the relationship. If you take someone for granted, they will eventually leave. Treat them poorly and they are as good as gone (mentally if not physically). If you treat someone like an option or a given, they may leave you for a choice of their own. Everyone has a choice. Just like you wouldn't settle being a benchwarmer for someone, you can't expect to treat someone as a "given" and expect them to be satisfied or fulfilled.

Relationships thrive on mutual choice and mutual respect. It's not enough to think of someone as your significant other, you must also acknowledge and demonstrate to them that they are significant in your life. It's a two way street requiring two committed partners.

Aloha means both goodbye and hello. If you truly want someone—want them now, not after they are gone.

"I didn't forget, I just remembered too late."

~ Michael

Open up and say aah.

Aah, innocence. Remember back in high school when you thought your boyfriend or girlfriend would be yours forever? You were absolutely captivated and enthralled and the very thought of that person gave you spine-tingling warm fuzzies. Are you innocent enough to be open to those feelings today? Are you still embracing life with wide-eyed zeal?

If your innocence feels lost, what will it take for you to break down those walls—just a brick at a time? Being jaded or innocent aren't necessarily exclusive of each other. Being cognizant and leery doesn't mean you can't be open and innocent. Perhaps innocence can signify something a bit different and changes with life experiences. Maybe things that feel innocent to you today seemed scandalous in your youth. Likewise, there are likely things you did back in the day that you'd never consider now that you are a "responsible adult."

What changed? What could you do with that abandoned, youthful innocence? Learning from the past helps you appreciate what the future holds. Seeing old things as fresh creates opportunities and possibilities long assumed lost. Are you willing to try? Arms wide open?

"Every act of rebellion expresses a nostalgia for innocence and an appeal to the essence of being."

~ Albert Camus

I'm parched. Do you have any water?

The opposite of love isn't hate, it's indifference. Hate is a hard emotion, carrying feelings just as deep as love. Indifference, on the other hand, means not caring one way or the other. In fact, indifference is the opposite of both love *and* hate. I may be indifferent about someone I've never met or a chair that is neither comfy nor hard on the back, but to a person that we are or have been close with, indifference is rare.

Let's look at it from another perspective. In business your biggest competitor may not be the store down the street or the person offering the same service as you. It may be simply that your prospects don't fully value your offering and just continue what they've always done. The, "meh, I've seen better," or, "why bother?"

Another example of indifference is found in the phrase, "Mailing it in." The definition of mailing it in? *To stop thinking about someone or something. To not care anymore.* Before you decide that you love or hate someone, check your emotional commitment.

Watch for relationship dialogue that migrates from thoughtful conversation to "sure," "whatever you want," "uh-huh," or "fine." Likewise, if you find yourself saying or hearing more and shorter, curt, blasé, off-hand comments or responses—those are persuasive signs of complacency and signal that it might be time to reboot your relationship. In this case, ignorance is not bliss. It's relationship suicide. Sure, no one can be 100% dialed in and focused 100% of the time. Just be cognizant and, if you don't feel engaged, try saying "I need a few minutes" and regroup.

Here's a real-life example: I was recently sitting in a coffee shop and I overheard a man—excited about something he was reading—say to his partner, "Check this out, it's so cool!" She replied, "Not interested. If you still want to show me tonight when you get home, fine." Reach your own conclusion. Why was he reading while she was staring absently through the green mermaid logo? Why didn't she care enough to give him a few seconds of time? There are many unknowns in this instance, but it caused me to ponder a fundamental axiom we would all do well to heed: *Never cause the one you love to feel alone—especially when you are there.*

It's one thing not to send a random card or a small gift when your partner and you are apart. You take it to entirely different level though if you ignore your partner when you are both in the same space. You have a finite amount of time and opportunity to share in each other. Play your video games or surf the net on your own time. Not on "we" time.

It's okay to take personal "me" time. It's important to take a time-out every now and then to recharge your batteries, recalibrate your thoughts, and do some self-discovery. Just make sure you take your partner into consideration and don't make it a 90 / 10 split in which you are mentally or physically checked out of your relationship most of the time. If you are both sitting quietly reading, great. But if your partner is just staring at a wall or playing with their fingernails—engage. No, it isn't your responsibility to be a source of continuous entertainment, but showing concern is always smart.

Healthy relationships have a lot in common with thriving, growing gardens. You can't simply throw seeds on the ground, walk away, and expect a bountiful harvest. You have to nurture, cultivate, and maintain it which involves repetitive tasks like weeding, watering, and fertilizing. But the reward of those delightfully aromatic flowers and plants, the succulent, fresh, clean flavor, and the pride of accomplishment far outweighs the ground work (pun intended). The same with your life relationships. Work and effort is required to produce the best tasting, organic, yummy food you've ever experienced. You can't be an absentee farmer and expect to win any prizes at the county fair.

Don't like something in your relationship? Talk. Want something? Ask. If you love someone—show them. If you don't, why are you there? Sitting around thinking about how much you love someone is like peeing in a pair of dark suede pants or slacks. It gives you a nice warm feeling but no one knows about it. Not showing someone you love them is like letting them die of dehydration when you have a case of bottled water sitting behind the couch.

"The worst sin towards our fellow creatures is not to hate them,
but to be indifferent to them; that's the essence of inhumanity."
~ George Bernard Shaw

Go to your room!

How do you use anger or fear to get your way? As a child you threw tantrums angling for special treats. As an adult, you might go off on a sales clerk to get your way. Perhaps you yell at employees so they'll work harder or faster. Or you ride your pick-up league softball teammates, pointing out every mistake, prodding them to do better.

All of these are examples of using emotions to get other people to behave either the way you want them to, or the way you expect them to. Your teammates probably want to become better players anyway (and resent your continual chatter). Your employees respond out of fear of losing their job and paycheck.

However, since fear and anger are emotions, they are also short-term motivators. When their effects ebb, so does the motivation. Eventually those on the receiving end of your tirades or pouting sessions will get resentful and fed-up and begin looking for another team or job.

Your partner will likewise not be motivated in those ways. Your partner *chooses* to be with you. Using fear, threats, or anger in an intimate relationship only drives a stake into the heart of what brought (and keeps) you together.

A common way people try to manipulate their partner's behavior is by using the timeworn standby, "If you *really* love me, you would ..." Maybe they are loving you, just not how you visualize it. Maybe you haven't communicated what causes you to feel loved. Will you recognize it when you have it? How?

So, who's keeping score? You know, "Look at everything I do for him / her. I, "a,b,c,d,e ..." rattling off how great and supportive you are. You find yourself thinking, "He doesn't love me as much as I love him." Or, "He doesn't care as much as I do or else he would (insert your personal checklist here)." And rather than talk it through, you sulk about it.

For starters, it's your responsibility to let the other person know what creates feelings of love for you. Someone doing dishes and taking out the garbage might make you feel cared for and loved, while in return, that person yearns for a simple hug and kiss. We each recognize and accept love on our own terms. You can't assume your terms are the same as anyone else's. Simply put, if I do the laundry, wash and gas up your car, mow the lawn, do the dishes, paint the house, but you just want to share meals together and have me home at 5:30pm after work—then you might not feel loved and I might be thinking, "What do I have to do around here?!"

During a recent lunch conversation, a friend expressed her frustration about the lack of romance in her relationship. I reminded her that romance is a two way street—give and take. A lifelong seduction. To this she replied, "Well, I like to be romanced, but I don't know how to be romantic." I mentally bounced that around, considering the variables and possibilities.

Maybe her relationship has become stagnant. Maybe she's just not that into him. Or maybe she really is being completely open. Perhaps she'd not been in a position to be, or assume the role of, the romantic leader. Maybe her significant other is always the aggressor. With no experience from that side of the equation; she would be a complete neophyte. There are many scenarios, and no "one size fits all" answer.

There are probably countless others out there in the same boat; those who may not believe they know how to be romantic. Even if they feel it, just might not know how to demonstrate it. They recognize it when they receive it, but don't know how to give it in return. Is it a fear of rejection? Being a creature of habit existing in their only known, familiar environment?

When it comes to giving and getting love, no matter how hard we try, none of us—you, me, your friend's girlfriend, your girlfriend's boyfriend—will be able to compete with the image locked in our own head.

If you do something you consider romantic but the recipient of your intentions doesn't recognize it as romantic, that's your signal to take time to get on the same wavelength. Having good intentions isn't always enough; you must also clearly communicate your desires. For instance, if you blindfold someone then stand behind them and ask them to trust you to catch them if they fall, then you better be certain they fall backwards.

Base your romantic gestures on what gives your partner a feeling of being loved. Not just what gives *you* the warm fuzzies. You can never know everything you think you know or all there is to know about another person (including your partner). Question your assumptions. You might *assume* your partner knows what you want or need (after all, you've been together forever), but you shouldn't assume that another person can anticipate your every want or need. At some point, you have to communicate those desires. Probably more than once. After all, we're all human and no human is perfect.

It helps to develop a working knowledge of what is important to your partner (*hint*: ask, watch, pay attention). Don't assume they know what you want or assume you know what they want. Eliminate the tantrums and mope-fests and learn to recognize the important things that bring about feelings of being loved and appreciated.

"Do not teach your children never to be angry; teach them how to be angry."

~ Lyman Abbott

Memory grenades.

Even if you've never heard of the term, you're likely familiar with the symptoms.

If you've experienced a failed relationship you'll recognize memory grenades as those sudden, "Oh, life can't go on. How did this happen?" emotional pangs that leave you feeling as though your world is imploding. Fortunately, those mental explosions don't have to bring up negative, "I miss him so much, why didn't this work out?" thoughts over and again. You have a choice.

What if those grenades reminded you of a contented, happy place in life? Of *positive* experiences within the relationship. Those things that rush a smile onto your face and you feel like Mary Tyler Moore throwing her hat in the air (look it up) in complete jubilation of life.

The good stuff does exist—you just choose to keep it locked away in your head—because it's easier to recall only the bad things. Even so, the memories of the needs or desires that were met (or that you hoped to have fulfilled) within the relationship still live in your head. And that's where you need to steer your emotions.

Failed relationships leave behind emotional rubble and a lot of rebuilding to do. Once you've worked your way through the stages of grief (denial, anger, bargaining, depression, and acceptance), give yourself permission to have one last good cry, make sure you've learned the lessons to be learned, and then focus on those learnings and the positive, happy times you shared. Life's too short to be miserable over someone who no longer holds that place in your heart. You don't have to loathe them or dislike them, or wish harm on them. You *do* need to let go of those negative feelings and move forward with contentment and peace.

Know too, that when you are experiencing an emotional grenade relating to a past relationship, focusing on positive feeling surrounding the person (who threw the grenade) may be difficult. It probably *will* be difficult. And that's okay. Invest your feelings in the positive memories and keep it constructive. Don't allow yourself to drown in a pool of loathing or self-pity. Your life continues. When love ends, love begins.

Things don't always work out as we plan, but they *are* always powerful learning experiences. Live in your present and expect a bright future. Be wise enough to recognize those that want to be part of that happy glow with you. You can't make someone love you. You can't permanently change or manipulate someone's feelings. Give your heart knowing that it may be broken, but also with the knowledge that you are loving and lovable.

Realistically, two people can love each other and even yearn for each other, but—as the saying goes—sometimes love just isn't enough. Don't give up. Remaining bitter or shell-shocked isn't the answer. Those grenades lead to a fresh beginning that brings you one step closer to your life desires.

"Even if I knew that tomorrow the world would go to pieces, I would still plant my apple tree."

~ Martin Luther

Newton was a smart fellow.

Are you navigating an obstacle course or a life course? You get to choose. Life is pitted with potholes. Do you go out of your way to avoid them, fill them in when you find them, or dig a few of your own? Here's a short quiz (*Hint*—your answers may well be "all of the above"):

- Does walking in sand slow you down or comfort you?
- Do crashing ocean waves frighten or exhilarate you?
- Are steep hiking hills tiring and strenuous or provide exercise and a better view?
- Is a chilly wind annoying or bracing and refreshing?
- Do you find rain to be wet and chilling or renewing and cleansing?

You get the picture. We habitually see what we want to see. Multiple people can witness a crime and each describe the suspect uniquely. Sometimes it's memory, sometimes it's the situation. For instance, someone walking alone two blocks from you may register differently than if they are walking with a group of people, because you have context. Walking solo, someone 6' 8" may not seem out of the ordinary. In a crowd, you'd likely remember them as "tall."

There are myriad examples, right down to a miniscule grain of sand. To you it may bring thoughts of a sun-splashed beach. It carries a completely different connotation to people surviving in a hunger-stricken desert region of the world.

This applies to everything that sparks emotion in you. Wet paint, infuriated drivers, and those little things that tweak you but also make you who you are. You have decisions to make, often on the fly. As example, you can spike your blood pressure by being irate at the guy who just cut you off in traffic, raise *their* blood pressure by flipping them off, do both, or do neither.

It's no different on the home front. Times are you'll be angry, frustrated, befuddled, or exasperated. But, you can also choose to be happy or content or forgiving or calm. Different situations, different reactions. Just take a few seconds to consider your potential reaction to another's action and also the potential reaction to something you initiate.

Newton's Third Law of Motion teaches us that for every action there is an equal and opposite reaction. It doesn't say that the reaction has to be of the same ilk. You get to make that choice. Before reacting to anger with anger, try and find the root of the negative emotion. Life is short. Don't make it shorter or more trying than it is. Share contentment.

"You can tell the size of a man by the size of the thing that makes him mad."

~ Adlai E. Stevenson

Don't forget to check the tire pressure.

How do (or would) you articulate your relationship with your significant other? Do you envision it chronologically (e.g. how long you have been together), by physical benchmarks (your first kiss, etc.), or by relationship milestones like anniversaries? Is it bundled by accomplishments, is it memories you've shared, or anticipation of things yet to come? Is it fresh off the showroom floor or a reliable, trusted vehicle?

Let's explore the vehicle analogy in more detail. Is it a lumbering truck or an agile, fast sports car? A minivan or SUV? Do you keep it in a garage or is it left sitting in the elements? Spotless and polished to a glimmering shine or rusted, dirty, and dusty? Is it brand spanking new or in its later years?

Keep in mind, there are immaculately conditioned vehicles from the early 20th century that are highly coveted by collectors and investors. Why? Scarcity. Like a treasured relationship, that one-hundred year old vehicle became the glint in an investor's eye by being well-maintained and shown due attention. Conversely, there are junk yards laden with tons of nearly new vehicles.

Dents can be repaired, paint can be waxed, scratches removed. It takes a little elbow grease. You get out of it what you put into it. Just like it takes more than staging periodic "date nights" to keep a loving relationship fresh. Date nights can be a relationship's tires but they're not the engine, and you can only coast so far and only when you're going downhill. Those special nights are worthwhile though, so don't wait until the tire's flat to put in air. Even then, fully inflated tires must be rotated, balanced, and checked for uneven tread wear. Pay attention. The tires are what stands between your butt and the pavement.

Thinking date night as the be-all and end-all is similar to inflating the tires then driving with a nearly empty gas tank; you won't be going far (except downhill). Does all of this seem like a lot of work? It is. But you bought the car.

"Another flaw in the human character is that everybody wants to build and nobody wants to do maintenance."

~ Kurt Vonnegut, Hocus Pocus

Don't judge, don't preach.

Our friends mean well. Most of the time. But when they are experiencing relationship challenges, friends are often seeking just one thing: agreement for their side of the story. You know, when they rant, "he or she is just a (insert your favorite expletive) and, I'm never speaking to him again!" Naturally, as their friend, they look for your agreement.

Tricky situation. You want to commiserate and reassure them that everything will be okay. But you may also disagree with their take on things. You have to walk the fine line of sticking to your beliefs while not adding fuel to the fire and making matters seem worse. Help your friend work to get through their momentary crisis—especially when they are of the mindset to play the blame game. After all, not all ships that take on water will sink. Help them stop taking on water and not continue ramming the iceberg (their other half).

Are they going to appreciate hearing your, "this too shall pass," speech while they're pissed off? Probably not. Are they going to think you have their back? Probably not during the heat of their battle. Will they respect you? Eventually—after things calm down.

Listening, without blindly agreeing, often leads one to believe you are taking another person's side of things. Make it clear that your intent isn't to take sides, but rather to be there for support. You ~~can't~~ should never fight your friend's battles for them. You might want to try to "fix" things. Don't.

Best advice? Don't judge, don't preach. Listen without interrupting and avoid the natural tendency to jump in and try to solve everything. Being a great listener does not mean you are providing tacit approval. In fact, if you believe you are being a great friend simply by blindly agreeing with everything she says, you could be in for quite the surprise.

Beware the backlash if your friend reconciles with her other half. She may suddenly wonder why you were trying to get them to break up while her partner will be wondering why you don't like him. Kiss the invitation to the summer BBQ goodbye.

" We're in a giant car heading towards a brick wall and everyone's arguing over where they're going to sit."

~ David Suzuki

How's your eyesight?

Cartoons make love seem easy. The male espies the female, his eyes bulge out to the sound of a thunderous AAHOOO-GAAAH horn, and his heart starts thumping through his shirt. In the real world though, can you afford to have a cartoon heart? Oh, we love the concept—one look and we're hopelessly, helplessly, longingly in lust ... er ... love.

If you believe that to be possible, here's a way to accelerate the process: be open to it—receptive but not desperate. Spend the time you'd spend looking for a mate on yourself. Time spent on you is time best spent. After all, if you don't enjoy your own company what makes you think anyone else will? Be comfortable in your own skin. Like yourself. No matter what else occurs in your life, you are the only one guaranteed to be there every moment of it. Making you the best you that you can is a most attractive quality (and attractive to others as well).

Sometimes people desire a relationship so much, or believe that to be whole they must be in a relationship, that they make poor choices based on that perceived need. One of the bands I used to play with performed in local bars. We used a shtick at closing time in which I'd announce, "It's that time of the night, folks. Where a guy looks across the room and sees the beautiful girl longingly looking back at him, and a voice, seemingly from heaven, says (and I lean closer into the mic and whisper) "last call." Smart choices are rarely made at that moment. But, I'm not one to judge. If it works for you, then, "bottoms up!"

When couples do have a romantic "love at first sight" beginning, they still face the challenge of falling in *like* with the other person. Perhaps the fantasy of it all can buy the time it takes for "like" to occur. But, like a tripod missing a leg, love at first sight, head-over-heels giddiness is a precarious place to alight with your eyes closed. The problem of "first sight" is it only lasts for that moment. The expiration date will hit you quick. Be ready for the work and make it worth the work.

" *Your task is not to seek for Love, but merely to seek and find all the barriers within yourself that you have built against it.*"

~ Rumi, thirteenth century Sufi poet

Harmony is a beautiful thing.

You've heard the saying about being on the same page with someone, or the musical equivalent—playing the same song in harmony. Even though we might be playing the same song, a lot of things still need to fall into place.

As example, let's say you and I have chosen a song to play together. You at the piano and me on guitar. You use sheet music and I'll use chord charts. We've agreed on the song. Check. We've agreed on the key. Check. We've agreed on the instruments. So what could possibly go wrong? Let's see ... tempo. Check. Volume. Check. It still sounds terrible. What's missing? Oh ... that's right—synchronization.

Playing the same song doesn't matter if I'm playing a different section than you. Nearly everything can go absolutely right, but just one little thing can still make everything go absolutely wrong.

It's not enough to glance at the song title and make assumptions about the result. Just like life. In his book, *Outliers: The Story of Success*, Malcolm Gladwell, in explaining his 10,000 hours rule, states that it takes roughly ten thousand hours of practice to achieve mastery in any given field. (To which I add that even 10,000 hours won't make much difference if you practice the same errors over and again.)

I'd venture to say that when applying a similar axiom to partner relationships and matters of the heart, we need to practice *at least* 10,000 hours of kindness, compassion, listening skills, forgiveness, honesty, and sincerity to fully possess the skills to healthily approach and appreciate the relationship. These skills should be considered prerequisites. Unfortunately, in life, we're sometimes forced to learn on the job. If you are in a position where you've no choice but to practice and hone your skills on the fly—dig in! It's never too late start logging some hours and lose the, "I don't know how" excuse.

Play your relationship music with complete synchronicity. It takes practice. If not, scores (no pun intended) of composers and conductors would be out of work and metronomes would be worthless. Use the tools and practice. Practice, practice, practice. You'll hit a few disjointed chords and flat notes along the way, but it's worth it. Harmony is a beautiful thing.

"Happiness is when what you think, what you say, and what you do are in harmony."

~ Mahatma Gandhi

You are one of billions.

It's a marketing axiom that the benefits, not the features, do the selling. In a nutshell, the WIIFM (what's in it for me) factor. But using that approach in personal relationships is ill-advised. It's okay to be a "confident go getter who knows what she wants." Just be careful not to cross the line to "narcissistic ass."

If you are always looking only to find what's in it for you, what makes you think anyone else should think differently about themselves? There's a brittle line between confidence and egomania and carrying around a sense of entitlement can backfire. All of us taking a "what's in it for me approach," is a sure way for none of us to get what we want out of a meaningful relationship.

Sure, it works in marketing. You need a hammer, I want to sell you a hammer. You get your needs met (hammer) and I get my needs met (cash/sale). But getting your needs met in a relationship without consideration of your partner's needs isn't really going to be productive in the long run.

Speaking of those needs—if you want to be sure you get what you pay for, it helps to know what you're shopping for. It's hard to point a blame finger at someone if you haven't done your basic homework. From personal relationships (are they emotionally available?), products (did you read reviews and warranties?), to jobs (is there growth opportunity?) and so on.

Though the saying, "you get what you pay for," is primarily geared towards the perceived quality of durable goods, it applies across your life spectrum. All your nouns, if you will.

Many negative experiences happen simply because ... wait for it ... we got *exactly* what we paid for. It pays to know what you are buying or getting into. Part of the WIIFM approach is performing due diligence. And part of executing your due-diligence should be concern for the long-term impact of your decision. Seeking common ground with a cohesive "we" attitude usually wins out over time.

As the common law of business balance reminds us—you can't pay a little and expect a lot in return. Paying a low sum may seem smart upfront, but it won't guarantee a high-quality outcome. The result lingers long after the price is forgotten. Of course, paying through the nose for something doesn't guarantee quality either. That's the chance you take. With relationships, there is a "cost of doing business" for everyone involved. And the day to day realities of life together remain long after lust fades. Do your homework (your potential partner is).

"*When you get what you paid for—make sure that you got what you paid for. No refunds, no exchanges.*"

~ Michael

The webs we weave.

"What the husband doesn't know won't hurt his wife," is a line from the 1942 film, *To Be or Not to Be*, starring Carole Lombard and Jack Benny. And while it might be true in the short run, the long-term odds are a bit risky.

Consider the toll that secrets have on both the keeper and the one in the dark. In (the above) quote, the wife will be living with a secret that, over time, can become a growing abscess. Perhaps it's a "minor infraction"—squirrelling away money—or something deeper that puts the relationship at immediate risk; an illicit affair perhaps. Either way, it will affect the wife's outlook, cloud her judgment, and make it easier to deceive in the future. The first time is always the most difficult. After that, rationalization becomes master and that first deceit is long forgotten.

It's also a huge assumption thinking that the husband will never know what he doesn't know. If he shows any modicum of interest for his wife, he will certainly notice her shifting subtleties and nuances.

I was once visiting a friend at his place. Though my friend maintained conversation with me I could sense his preoccupation with the work-related phone conversation his girlfriend was having in another room. I finally asked him what the matter was. He replied that his girlfriend seemed unusually "friendly" on her call. I responded that I couldn't make out a thing that was being said in the other room. He replied that he couldn't either—that it was nothing he could put a finger on, just that her voice, her tone, and her inflection was *different* than usual. I asked if he really felt he was sensing that without hearing a word being said. He responded that he was certain of it.

Our conversation stayed with me and bounced around in my head for some time. Later that summer, she broke-up with my friend and began dating her new boss who was hired right around the time of the call I was describing. Coincidence? Maybe. I'll never know. I know that I wouldn't want to be in a relationship where I felt it necessary to worry about those things happening. I also wish not to live with my head in the sand.

That he sensed something off or different in that call stuck with me. I guess no one really knows a person until you've spent time with them on multiple levels in different settings. A side lesson here is to not judge a book by its cover or even by the first few chapters.

Secrets—large or small, financial, illicit, or innocent—usually reveal themselves. If nothing else, the deception involved will be enough to bite you right on the ass. And those remaining secrets eat you from the inside out like time-release poison.

Deciding not to divulge a secret is usually easy, while the opposite—not so much. But secrets become barriers; especially in intimate relationships. Not doing something you can't share is the easy solution and a good rule of thumb. Unfortunately, secrets and little white lies are part of life. Maybe you went out for a few beers when you said you'd be at work. Or your new earrings cost $400 but you confessed to the "extravagant" cost of $75.

Those little secrets seem innocent and you justify them by convincing yourself it's no big deal. In the long run though, keeping secrets to avoid an argument or confrontation usually backfires. Secrets represent a lack of trust. If you are hiding something or someone or choices you are making, you are eroding the foundation successful relationships build on. Secrets deny you the freedom of being who you are and sharing your fears and concerns with your partner. You lose the right to be respected for *who you are* if you deny your partner the right to know *who that is.*

It's not a question of can you keep a secret or even if you should keep secrets. It's deciding whether you can live with the consequences of either choice. And if not, take a step back and examine how you got into position of having a secret in the first place.

The bottom line: Secrets diminish physical and emotional intimacy as well as the trust we covet so much that we thought we were willing to lie to keep it.

"We swallow greedily any lie that flatters us, but we sip only little by little at a truth we find bitter."

~ Denis Diderot

Heart science.

Life often gets in the way of life. It's easy to flip the switch and start each morning in auto-mode. Shower, dress, eat, commute, work, home, change clothes, TV, sleep. Repeat for thirty or forty years. What's missing? Your life. Important people. Your husband, wife, significant other, kids, parents, friends, relatives ... important people. But we let life get in the way of living.

Here's an easy exercise for your romantic relationship. Complete these simple statements and then ask your partner to (independently) do the same. Answer with the first thing that comes to mind.

When I see my partner the first time of any given day ...

- The first thing I think is ...
- The first thing I say is ...
- The first thing I do is ...
- When my child(ren) are heading out to school, I say ...
- I get into bed after a long day. I turn to my partner (if applicable) and ...
- My Mom/Dad or other significant just called. The last thing I said before we hung up was ...

When you both have finished, compare your results with those of your partner. Notice the commonalities? The differences? You'll probably find things that surprise one of you, along with answers that show where you presently have different priorities. Mind you, this isn't a "gotcha!" exercise, or an opportunity to blurt out, "see,

297

you don't care as much as I do." You are simply taking a snapshot of where you are mentally at any given time.

Sometimes the first thing you think of *will* be your job or bills or a dental appointment. It is possible though to be thinking about those people important in your life (including yourself) as your daily priorities are shifting. *Life happens.* It doesn't mean you're selfish. Maybe one of you is really stressed about work right now while the other is micro-focused on school, kids, or maybe even your romantic time together. Just use the tool for what it is—a periodic gauge of where you each are at any given moment. It's an easy, effective, and straight forward learning tool.

It's also a reminder to never lose focus of those people important in your life. It's not about acceptance or finding your inner self (though that may be a side dynamic). Here, it's about sustaining deep, loving relationships. With others and within yourself. It isn't rocket science. It's *heart* science.

"When your life is on the go; take your life with you."

~ Michael

Animal Magnetism.

It's interesting the love, attention, and affection we show our pets, yet often choose to maintain a steel-hardened shell around us when interacting with humans. I get the argument that pets love us unconditionally (*so long as we care for them and show them love and affection*), and that dogs don't know if we've been gone for fifteen minutes or fifteen days (*with love, time comes to a standstill*), and are always elated to see us and shower us with affection. (*Seriously, where's my treat?*)

If your cat squawked-up her din-din, leaving a nice piece of gooey rope on your carpet you'd be mad as hell. *But*, you'd clean it up and just as quickly as she crawls into your lap (*your lap was empty and inviting*), all would be forgiven (*you took care of it*). When it comes to our human relationships, conditions apply. Maybe it's because the people in your life aren't as amiable as your pet. Lesson? Be willing to forgive, forget, and be as ebullient to see your partner as you are the cat.

By the way; take note of the items in parentheses. It's not only animals that have those desires ...

"Everyone wants someone to believe in them—even if they're pretending; and everyone needs to believe that someone believes in them."

~ Michael

Oh, there are conditions all right.

"I love you unconditionally." My spidey senses call B.S. on this one. Someone may say, "I love you unconditionally," but there's almost always a catch.

Maybe love itself can be unconditional, but love isn't the only emotion involved in this equation. We also want trust, respect, security, pride, loyalty, honesty, support, connection, and countless other things. So is it physically possible to be with another person, professing unconditional love, without other components? Sure, I may love my mother unconditionally, but it doesn't mean I want to spend my life with her. Or I may tell someone my deepest, darkest secret and trust them with it explicitly, but it doesn't mean I unconditionally love them.

Similarly, those who have ended a committed relationship and then find themselves migrating back to their ex, soon recognize the additional boundaries imposed by both parties. And boundaries are conditions. So, by definition, that is not unconditional love. If your partner steps outside the relationship, and then wants to reconcile—you might say, "Yes, *but if this happens again,* it's over," thus placing another (not unreasonable) condition on the relationship.

The take-away? You can reduce or lessen the severity of the conditions, but you probably won't find yourself in a romantic relationship with zero conditions (not to be confused with zero-based affection). Ultimate example? Christianity tells those who read the Bible: *For God so loved the world that he gave his one and only Son, that whoever believes in him shall not perish but have eternal life* (John 3:16). Even God has conditions.

The sooner you accept and decide which conditions are a 1 (not that big of deal) or a 10 (absolute deal breaker), the better you'll both be. But whether a 1 or a 10—they are *all* conditions. Go in being respectful of that.

"*We are who we are both because of, and regardless of, who we were.*"

~ Michael

Forget about forgetting.

You may be a kind, sensitive, forgiving person, but I'll bet you dollars to donuts that you never forget a serious affront. Forgiving is a process; sometimes painful and difficult, often lengthy. Forgetting, on the other hand, is nearly impossible. And personal relationships are prime real estate for the "forgive and forget" merry-go-round.

While seemingly perfect partners, forgetting and forgiving are distinct animals. It's impossible to make a conscious decision to simply forget something, even something which we might graciously choose to forgive. Naturally, this little lack of forgetfulness can lead to mistrust, hesitancy, fear, and reluctance to connect on an intimate level.

At some point, everyone makes mistakes and hurts the ones they love. And if hurtfulness becomes status quo, forgiveness weakens. Focusing on forgetting can lead to suppressing feelings about the wrong; and that's not the same as forgiving. Forgiveness happens when you are able to remember the wrong without feeling resentment. Even so, you'll always remember.

Unlike forgetting, forgiveness is a powerful *choice*. Forgiveness does not minimize, justify, or excuse the wrong. Forgiveness also does not mean denying the harm and the feelings that the injustice produced.

Along this path, we don't have to forget in order to forgive. And just to keep it interesting, here's another reason you shouldn't fret about forgetting: The lessons. Some encroachments are blatant, cut and dry infractions. If a loved one was killed by a driver under the influence, I might, over time, forgive. Certainly though, I will never, would never want to forget the person I'd lost.

With other situations, there could be gray areas with little nuggets of learnings to be sifted and mined. Forgive if, when, and how you see fit, but forget about forgetting and get on with the lessons and the teachings. Remember too, there'll inevitably be times when it's you that seeks forgiveness.

"*When you forgive, you in no way change the past – but you sure do change the future.*"

~ Bernard Meltzer

Save some love for me!

Fairly or not we compare everyone in our lives to everyone in *life*. In your loving relationship you are unconsciously (likely for both of you) competing with every point of contact your partner has. From their dry cleaner, coffee house, favorite restaurant, or clothing shop. Don't believe it? Let's take a hypothetical walk through a typical day.

You get up in the morning, make your usual coffee stop where the barista greets you by name—your nonfat, no-foam jolt already in the works. Expensive, but they are great folks and, hey, you're worth it. Then you swing by the dry cleaner where the owner—having seen you pull into the parking lot—has your freshly cleaned, pressed, and wrapped items hanging on the rack waiting.

Driving into work, traffic is tight. It's hot and muggy and you're craving the office air conditioning. An agreeable motorist stops and waves you into traffic after you'd been idling at a non-signal side street for an eternity. You give a wave of "thanks" and receive the "no problem" wave in return. A considerate stranger.

Arriving at the office, you give a quick call to your partner and see how their day is getting on. Your expectations have already been set by places and people they may not even know. In one case, a complete stranger.

Well, they're really busy (you understand). Don't really have time to talk (totally get it). Need to get their car to the shop ASAP (got it). "Maybe talk later, K?" "click." Totally not getting it. You'd have valued a conversation of the same length that went something like, "Hi, honey. I am swamped this morning. So frustrating. I hope you are having a great morning. I can't wait to see you tonight! I love you." How long would that have taken—ten seconds? The bar had already been set by strangers and now is being terribly missed by the one person you turn to and care about the most. And he may not even realize it.

We put on our best face for strangers (politeness), for customers (money and loyalty), and co-workers (success, promotion, and stability). The special person we look to for those things in life? Well, as the partner, you're expected to understand and not be "needy." Problem is, we all *do* need that politeness, loyalty, stability, time, and love—*especially* from our partner.

~ *Take the time and take the time.* ~

The chair test.

One warm summer evening my other half and I opted to make dinner on the outdoor grill. To get a head start, I cleaned the grill, scrubbed a couple spuds, then picked and rinsed a few handfuls of strawberries and raspberries from our garden patch.

Through her open office window, the lady of the house asked, "Can you please give me a hand?" She wanted to move a chair from one room to another. I slipped in through the patio slider and met her outside her office door where she had an upholstered armchair tilted awkwardly on its side, attempting to squeeze it through. I flipped the cushion off the chair to make for an easier move. She looked at me and, with an unmistakable touch of derision, said, "Well, that's a start," thinking I'd been lazing around in the living room watching TV while she was busy working and was now giving her the brush off.

She wasn't aware of what I'd been doing, only that I wasn't meeting *her* immediate need nor in the manner that she'd hoped. In turn, I was frustrated because I'd been diligently prepping our dinner. It was a prime example of how not knowing what you don't know can impact situational dynamics. It wasn't a lack of communication. It wasn't an act of anger. We simply didn't know what each other was up to. Ignorance isn't always bliss. Often, it doesn't matter what you do, but what the other person *believes* you are doing and how it affects them. I failed the chair test.

" *We don't see things as they are, we see things as we are.*"

~ Anaïs Nin

Me, me, me!

From an enjoyable time at the beach to a blistering sunburn, a pleasant dip in the pool to wrinkled fingers; it's possible to have too much of a good thing.* Addiction aside, how does too much of a good thing apply in everyday life? For instance, most of us have a friend (or two) whom we adore who has an uncanny ability to talk without pausing for breath. You love 'em, but a little goes a long way (Dear Lord, please ... breathe!).

Where is that elusive, fuzzy line in a partner relationship? The line that separates, "I can't wait to see him," from, "I wish he would go watch a football game or something." A harbinger that it's time for a "me" break. When it's me time—take it. Don't wait until you're resentful.

One of the simplest, yet most difficult ways to gain some personal time is by saying no. Most of us have a natural tendency to want to be helpful and pull our own weight or show others how smart, useful, or indispensable we are. Fact is though, the more you do, the less effective you will become at all of it and the more frazzled you'll feel.

Go ahead and take fifteen minutes. An hour. A weekend. You'll realize what's too brief or too long, and what's perfect to recharge your "me" batteries. Start with something easy. Schedule time on your calendar—even if just thirty minutes or an hour—and treat it as you would any other commitment.

What should you do? Whatever you want—it's your meeting! Read. Meditate. Take a nap. It doesn't matter. You might feel awkward, bored, lonely, or even guilty at first. That's okay. You need to take time to separate from life's constant barrage of tugs, wants, to do lists, and everyone else's "me, me, me" demands. Put yourself on a list, even if the list has just that one (important) goal—"me."

* For the curious: laboratory tests confirm that wrinkly fingers improve our grip on wet objects, working to channel away water like rain treads in car tires. (Source Nature magazine, January 9, 2013.)

"*When we cannot bear to be alone, it means we do not properly value the only companion we will have from birth to death—ourselves.*"

~ Eda LeShan

Is it really that important?

"This is going to bother me ... right up to when I forget about it."

How many times have you been upset about something only to altogether forget about it in an hour (or a day or a week)? Well, that was a lot of gut-wrenching negative emotion distilled and consumed for nada. We realize that letting go of negative emotion is healthy. The challenge though is doing so. We get so caught up in having to be right or needing to win that it becomes a grand obsession. Sometimes, it doesn't matter who is right or who is wrong. What may be central is its perceived importance to you.

You must decide if you want to win the battle or the war. On your scale of 1 to 10, where 1 represents, "matters not," and 10 is, "this means the world to me," choose wisely. Take a step back and ask yourself, "Is this a 3 or a 10?" If it is a 10, address it. Often it is a 1 or 2 but we get caught up in the minutiae of things. "I told you to not tuck in the sheets." "I told you to gas up the car!"

Never lose site of the end game. Take in the entire picture and choose your battles thoughtfully, keeping in mind what it is you are trying to achieve. You might find that when all is said and done that saying less will get more things done. Make sure it registers as a 9 or 10 to you before going into full-on guerrilla mode. Learn to let go. "If it's not a ten, let it blend."

Remember too, that if everything is a 2 or 3 for you and a 9 or 10 for your partner (or co-worker, boss, friend, etc.), your opinion may not carry much weight. When something is important to you, you'll need the self-confidence to trust in your opinion, and the courage to articulate them in a calm, non-confrontational voice. If you never care, it's easy to get pushed around. It's critical to know if the other involved party is looking for a mutually desirable outcome and not just trying to continue an "I'm right, again!" winning streak. Here are a few tips on dealing with Mr./Ms. (always) Right:

- Keep calm (even when it's a 10).
- Seek common ground—something you can both agree on within the scope of the discussion.
- Stick to the facts.
- Look for solutions, not "game points."
- Recognize when a discussion is getting out of control (anger, finger pointing, abusive language), and don't be afraid to end the discussion and continue it another time.

It might feel good to win your point, but a mutually beneficial result is usually the better solution.

"Some people seem to look for ways to overcome happiness. And surprise, surprise: their success rate is a perfect 100%."

~ Michael

What did you appreciate today?

"We didn't do anything 'extra' or anything to make each other feel special."

Few come right out and say it like that. As often as not, it's something more along the lines of, "He didn't do anything to make me feel special."

Most of us are well versed in pointing out things that annoy us, especially in the people we're closest to. Whether it's your habitually late partner, your mess-a-minute children, or those slacking co-workers. Unfortunately, research shows that it takes (*at minimum*) five positives to equal one of those negatives. So here's my challenge for you: Find reasons to give encouraging affirmation. And if you can't find anything, I'd venture you aren't looking.

About all those negatives. Is it really going to help to point out to your partner that she came home ten minutes late? Wouldn't it be better for your relationship to share how happy you are to see him? Save the inevitable negatives for the really important issues. Try using the previously discussed 1 to 10 scale (where 1 is a "meh, whatever, let's move on," and 10 being something that can continually affect the relationship in a negative way).

This applies across all relationships, not just with your partner. Have children? Okay, so they came home with a stain on a new shirt. Is that the end of the world? No. It might be a learning opportunity, but it's certainly not the apocalypse. Same with co-workers. Was it simply irksome (a 1-5), or a critical disagreement (6 –10) that needs discussion? Nothing here suggests that you be a pushover. Not by any means. Just consider if you are improving or eroding a situation within the scope of the relationship.

Before pointing out the negatives (hey—we're human), stop for a second and give yourself an opportunity to learn new ways of thinking and adapting to the ways of others. You'll be glad you did (and so will the others in your life).

~ Tradeoff + Compromise = Adaptation ~

Teamwork 101

The Star Cycle Company of Wolverhampton, England, introduced its Combination Roadster tandem bicycle in 1896. It had a link from the rear set of handlebars to the front fork. This enabled the person sitting in back to steer the bike. (Perhaps the original back seat driver—with serious authority!) This bike required a unique set of teamwork skills and the ability to work together in achieving a common goal (destination sans bruises and road rash). It could easily deteriorate into a comedy of errors.

"You push, I'll pull."

"No, *you* push, I'll pull."

"Let's both push."

"Then who'll steer?"

Though that might sound like an old comedy routine, for many couples it's probably all too familiar, and not very amusing. Lesson—you don't have to agree on everything but you need to find common ground on the important matters. Nothing makes for a shorter tandem bike trip to the beach than one person turning left with the other attempting to turn right.

What are the secrets of successful teams? It's not rocket science, but, even so, everyone is a genius at something. Discovering what your gift is and leveraging it is pretty smart in itself. And recognizing the genius of your other half really fuels the creative, collaborative fire. In a relationship, no person is always more significant or of more value than their partner; just as no job is entirely independent of others. The pilot is lost without navigation. The navigator is of little value without the cartographer. The cartographer needs the surveyor. And so it goes. Finding your inner-genius and surrounding yourself with the complementary pieces is both an act of genius and a valuable lesson in humility. After all, if you judge a fish by its ability to climb a tree, it'll live its (brief) life believing it's stupid.

Okay, we've determined that your partner and you are both Mensa poster models. So, who's going to be the boss? If you are having that conversation: Stop. Take a breath and tell yourself, "There is no boss around here." Sure, in all partnerships occasionally one person will need to take control and use their individual strengths and abilities to best resolve a situation. But for one person to consider themselves "the boss" is like tossing anger and resentment into a boiling cauldron of water. It's not going taste good, it's going to be messy, and someone is going to get burned.

While a life relationship requires effort and work, it is *not* a work relationship. It's a partnership with equal ownership in the business of life. You can't build a home you want to live in for fifty years by taking shortcuts during construction. It takes craftsmanship and attention to detail. As the saying goes, "built with love." The challenges will be there, just as they are in professional partnerships.

In work relationships, all things being equal (and they seldom are), little gets done when everyone has equal voting rights. An impasse may occur and we all know where that can lead; dissolution of the partnership or a hunt for a new partner. From a strict business perspective, a successful 50/50 decision making model is rare. There is a boss. Whether that's what they are called or not. You've probably heard (or experienced) that if you want to push something to the back burner, form a committee. It'll be rehashed forever, without action. But even committees have chairpersons.

Back on the home front, how can you address the conundrum of having everything be 50/50 and still achieve mutual goals? You can start by making a list: What do you like to do, and conversely, dislike? What chores rank as "no biggie" and what do you avoid at all costs? As example, for me—mowing the lawn, raking, trimming—are chores I don't mind. I gain a sense of accomplishment and get a bit of exercise. I also don't mind doing dishes, laundry, or taking out garbage. Making a bed, however? Whole other story. I'd as soon sleep on the couch. As part of the partnership with my other half, the lawn stays mowed and I sleep in a nice, freshly made bed. This isn't as business-like as it may first seem. We simply determined individual likes and toleration levels for various tasks. By so doing, we found that things naturally fell into place.

Of course, there'll be things that neither of you particularly enjoy, as well as stuff in which you both gain satisfaction. No neurosurgery required here. Both of you enjoy it? Do it together. Both disdain it? Take turns. If you can't decide who should do something, decide using another criteria. For instance, who does it better? Or for whom is it more convenient? (Here comes another argument, I can smell it brewing—but hang with me here.) As example, if the trash collector comes by early Tuesday mornings, perhaps the last person home Monday evening should take the trash bin to the curb. Likewise, the first person home Tuesday evening should retrieve the empty container.

All this may seem incredibly basic, but when everyone has a clear understanding of who does what, when, and why—it works. It's when you attempt to dictate the "how" that you'll run into trouble. Do it yourself or keep your lips zipped.

Some things will be resolved by need or desire. The car breaks down. You didn't plan for it, but you need your partner to pick you up. Or maybe it's motivated by desire—you buy a large piece of unassembled furniture and your other half may not physically be able to help build it.

Now to the communication challenges. The, "I'll do it later," or, "I'm tired," or (insert your favorite excuse here). So, now, we're going to install some logic and ground rules. Ready? Here it is: You are responsible for X. It needs to be accomplished by Y. X + Y = happy happy joy joy. The penalty for not keeping up your end of the bargain? Living with the knowledge (and miserable feeling) that you are letting your partner down by showing a lack of respect and disregard for an agreement you've committed to. If stuff matters, it matters. If it doesn't, then take it off the list and forget about it.

This isn't a chore list for a weekly allowance. It's a lifetime partnership list with the goal of eliminating the finger pointing and reducing the frustrations of everyday life. What are the potential repercussions? Major. It's not a time out or no TV for the night. It's your relationship. Besides, knowing that there are some rules provides flexible, fluid components. Without need to worry or argue about who is doing dishes or mowing the lawn, you can focus on the positive, fun things you enjoy sharing.

Remember, it's not about giving in. It's mutual give and take. Reciprocity. That doesn't mean keeping a score card of everything you've done and waving it in your partner's face. Sometimes it's as basic as getting off your high-horse, shedding the body armor and dropping the lance. Live to joust another day. It's good for the relationship. At the end of the day, it's about not degenerating into a huge power struggle. Don't let it erode into a "he-said, she-said" battle. Nurture a "we said" mentality.

"When your relationship is important, one plus one equals three."

~ Michael

Backup Behavior.

Those things we do when we don't get what we want or when things don't go the way we want them to. There are numerous catalysts that can spur an onset of backup behavior. Stress, frustration, fright, being backed into a corner, or fear are among the most common.

Outward manifestations include being quiet or refusing to talk, yelling, slamming fists on a table top, or sulking. No matter how much we might look down on such behaviors, we all carry them around inside of us and act them out in our own way. It's easy to deduce the backup behavior of a small child—crying or stomping, holding their breath, or screaming. It's demonstrated multiple ways by adults as well—from being sullen, working behind other's backs, plotting revenge, and yes, some yelling and stomping.

Ironically, most of us are more likely to control our backup tendencies at work or around strangers or casual acquaintances and save both our best and our worst for those we care about the most. You'd not likely sulk off into the corner of a conference room during a meeting if things didn't go your way, but have no problem at home slamming a door and stomping off into another room under similar circumstances.

The more familiar you are with someone, the more you likely know about their perceived shortcomings. This makes finding fault easier and creates a larger likelihood of acting out your backup behaviors in their presence. Because, after all, they have faults, you're perfect, and that's that. You'll hold your breath until they see the light. So there!

Everyone wants to get their way, but real growth requires seeing other points of view even when convinced of our own certainties. Some believe it's their way or the highway, while others think there are two sides to every story. I'm of the belief that there are *at least* two sides to every story. See, you don't have to agree on everything. It is important, however, to recognize and acknowledge your significant other's abilities and contributions. Successful partners recognize and agree on the important goals and work together—in tandem—to achieve them.

" We don't remember who was standing on first, second, or third base. Rarely, who scored the lead run. But always which team won."

~ Michael

Just because.

Let's revisit the old saying, "If you always do what you've always done, you'll always get what you've always got." While that might hold true a small percentage of the time in other aspects of life, from a relationship perspective, it doesn't hold water. Life relationships continually evolve and require an enduring, renewing commitment.

We're incessantly growing, learning, and being influenced by life around us. The only way nothing would change would be to live in a cave and lead a solitary existence without outside influence. Even then, you'd learn to adapt to your conditions, and you'd continue to age and change physically. Changing, growing, and adapting is healthy, smart, and nearly impossible to avoid. Just don't leave behind everything that got you where you are.

For instance, many of us don't bother to do the little things we did early on. We catch our target (mate) then fall into a routine. While your partner (or you) is longing for those deep-rooted words, poems, songs, feelings, picnics—*love* things—one of you (or both) may think it's no longer necessary. It was never *necessary*. When it becomes a "have-to" it will fester into *resentment*.

Romancing someone and then letting it fall into disrepair is analogous to making a monetary 401K or IRA investment and then ignoring it with the assumption it'll take care of itself. Emotional needs require as much attention as financial needs. In both, strategies change, evolve, and grow. You have to stay on top of things, nurture the process, and monitor your relationship barometer. You've made an emotional investment. Ask yourself— what originally made you fall for this person? What was your investment goal? To grow, it requires nourishment and attention. It's lust to love or lust to bust.

You may be thinking, "Even if I make every possible effort, it'll eventually just become the same old thing—the new ordinary." Only if you let it. Each day provides a fresh opportunity to bring uplifting touches to the special person in your life. It doesn't have to be a new car or a trip to an exotic locale. Doesn't even have to cost money. Do something original, splash in some favorites (those love notes or cards you used to send spring to mind), and create your own magic. There is a never-ending supply of ideas and possibilities. Use your imagination! Which brings us to the magic of *just because.*

When was the last time you surprised your partner with a simple love note or card? Not talking about herculean effort here either. In just a minute or two you can send a free online card. Or every now and again, how about leaving a simple note in their purse, folio, or on their desk? For motorists, perhaps a surprise in their car or under the wiper blade of the windshield. Any of these would take just minutes of your time but would demonstrate your love to the recipient. Give it a try. But don't do it because you feel you have to. Do it *just because.*

"Friendship is two-sided. It isn't a friend just because someone's doing something nice for you. That's a nice person. There's friendship when you do for each other. It's like marriage – it's two-sided."
~ John Wooden

I love you.

Is "goodbye" a seven letter dirty word? People tell me, "Always say goodbye, it's the polite thing to do." I usually advocate the opposite.

Here's the thing. Do you want to have a phone conversation with that special someone and end it with "goodbye"? How about, "I love you," or, "I can't wait to see you." I know there are many people (*stereotypically* males) thinking this is stupid. "Just say goodbye and hang up already." Not to be macabre, but if that call were to be the last opportunity you had to talk with them, wouldn't you want to know that the last words they heard from you are, "I love you?"

You can say goodbye to a situation. To a bad experience. To a lousy job. You can tell your friends that you'll miss them as they are moving away. You can say goodbye to frizzy hair or acne or wrinkled shirts. You can find closure with past memories by putting them to bed and saying goodbye. But in your loving, life relationships—why say goodbye? "I love you," is always your better choice.

"Never say goodbye because goodbye means going away and going away means forgetting."

~ J.M. Barrie, Peter Pan

The special stuff.

Pondering an important life relationship? To stay or go? Fight or flight? Either way, devour the lessons. They might save a relationship or help keep another on track. If you don't learn the hard lessons–you take all the baggage with you when you pack.

Not every relationship will last a lifetime (none in its current iteration). Are you considering making a relationship change? Don't let it become, "I wish I would have, I sure could have, why didn't I," internal conversation that loops through your head the rest of your life. Sometimes you need to find another door and sometimes you need to walk back through the door that's right behind you.

Make informed decisions, being cognizant that life is pliable. And when you make a significant life choice, sleep well knowing you made the best decision you could with the information you had. Life is a continuous series of decisions, opportunities, challenges, and choices. Remember–contentment can include letting go of the past and looking forward to a magnificent future. Expect a positive and exciting life and commit to it. Not all things are, "once in a lifetime finds." Sometimes it is just a warehouse filled with stuff that you have to sort through on your search for the *special* stuff. Never stop discovering.

"The problem with having one foot in and one foot out is that you'll eventually lose your balance."

~ Michael

Time to fly!

Hooray—you survived. That wasn't too difficult, was it? Hopefully, you learned a few tips and gathered some ideas that you can put into use within your important relationships.

This brings us back to the very reason for this book—*you*. Let's now take a look at a few topics that will bring us full circle. Some food for thought and a few small reminders demonstrating how you *will* achieve, maintain, and live the fulfilling, purposeful, and loving life you desire.

Let your spirit soar!

"The essence of a tragedy, or even of a serious play, is the spiritual awakening, or regeneration, of the hero."
~ Maxwell Anderson

Horse? What horse?

You're probably familiar with the expression, "closing the barn door after the horse is gone," referring to an attempt to change something after it has already occurred (and thus can't be changed). The lesson here is that it's wiser and easier to tackle challenges as they surface, or better still, anticipate them as best you can and (to employ another metaphor), "get your head out of the sand." Sure, at times, we all hesitate or act a bit indecisively. Just as frequently though, we can be so stubborn and closed minded that we slam and lock the barn door without ever getting wind of a horse.

The most desirable traits to employ are to be evenhanded, impartial, and unbiased. Always easier said than done, and nearly impossible if everything is either a no or a yes. Open or shut.

You have to keep the barn door open for opportunity and new experiences. Yes, with the door open there is a chance the horse is going to run. But slamming it shut afterwards pretty much guarantees a couple things: The horse can't come back, and nothing new can get in. Stay opened minded. Don't die wondering. Give life a chance.

"Don't close the barn door until you've given the horse a chance to

run free."

~ Michael

It's coming.

What will you do when *it* happens? Because *it* will happen. Whatever it is and whenever it arrives. How can you prepare for something when that something is an unknown? We plan for assumed life events—retirement, college, and the like—but we can't plan for everything that may actually happen in life. "It" (whatever *it* is), is out there. Waiting.

Begin with this stark realization: you're going to die. We live here on earth forever. Until we don't. In fact, you just came a few moments closer to death while reading that. How can you prepare for this mystery? Great question, and life's most difficult questions sometimes simply don't have an answer that satisfies everyone. I imagine that your answer is different from mine and mine different from my neighbor's and so on. It's our individual perception of reality that creates our answer to those things otherwise left unanswered. So ... what is your "*it?*"

Perhaps Winston Churchill had it right in 1939 when speaking about Russia as, "a riddle wrapped in a mystery inside an enigma." Or as I say, "it" may be hidden to you now, but will eventually happen. And what a wonderful, often mysterious, journey. Stay open to life as it unwraps itself to you. It won't be there forever.

"Anyone who says that life is 10% what happens and 90% of how you react has never been dead."

~ Michael

Drop fear. Pick up some memories.

Replacing your fear of the unknown with the wonder of curiosity is a goal of audacity. Fear is a four letter word, and if you let it, fear will own you. Curiosity will set you free. Don't fear what you believe might happen. Look around. There's a whole world just waiting for you to discover and explore. The sooner you stop letting fear control you, the sooner you start living. Whether you have a day, a week, or a hundred years remaining, go to bed every night with joy and satisfaction of having discovered or learned something new. That you created memories that will last a lifetime. That's key to living a rich life.

Maybe you bring something home from your adventures. A wave and sand carved rock from a sun-drenched beach. An eagle feather from a hike on a rugged mountain trail. Those anchors will ignite your memory and you can relive those moments as often as you choose. They don't have to be physical mementos. Who doesn't remember the smell of fresh cut grass, or burning leaf piles in autumn (or diesel exhaust for my Chicago, NY, and LA readers)? All markers representing times of your life. Leave fear behind and let your curiosity create a treasure-trove of "life." Start your collection now.

"Satisfaction of one's curiosity is one of the greatest sources of happiness in life."

~ Linus Pauling

Life is *your* adventure.

Sometimes you have to grab the bull by the horns and wrestle it to the ground. To take some initiative and give yourself permission to live. Stop waiting for someone to tell you what to do, how to do it, and how to live your life. Their time would be better spent living their own. You'll never discover your passion(s) if you are too busy trying to help others live theirs.

Work on your own list—make your own discoveries. It's not that you will enjoy everything you try, but the living is in the doing, discovering things that have you anticipating each new day and every new opportunity. You won't find them looking through someone else's eyes. And if you wait for someone to give you permission, you may never get it. We are all motivated by a "me" mentality. Unless it fits into another person's vision of "yes," they won't have any reason or motivation to give you permission or to even care.

This whole thing should be called *life*. It's called *adventure* simply because so few of us live. Go! You're somewhere out there waiting for you. Life is to be cherished and embraced. Along the way, give yourself permission to let go of what you can't change. Fight the good fight knowing that sometimes it's okay to drop your sword and move on. Things don't always play out according to plan. Embrace uncertainty and don't allow it to rule your life. Harness its power and relish the unexpected adventures that come along with it.

Take a few minutes and reflect how wonderful and blessed life is. When was the last time you sat on a beach or by a stream or at a picnic table in a park and let your imagination take over? Life doesn't always have to be a continuing series of struggles, internal battles, and confrontations. Remember, nightmares are a part of dreaming. Put down your weapons (guilt, anger, fear) and just be. If there's one certainty, it's that life will continue to be uncertain. Enjoy the wealth of it all. As Greek philosopher Socrates stated, "The secret of change is to focus all of your energy, not on fighting the old, but on building the new."

"An ounce of adventure is worth a pound of permission."

~ Michael

Lights. Camera. *Action*!

Enter, stage left. It's your time to shine in the role of your lifetime. But this isn't a movie; you're playing you and it's real life, without a net, without rehearsals, and with oodles of ad-lib.

It's the process, the journey, the change. Nothing stays constant. Life is about adapting to change, facing challenges, and greeting opportunity. Each of us strives to come into our moment, our glory. To grab our fifteen minutes of fame. Relax and enjoy the adventure, knowing that everything will be right. Even if you don't win (a term we all define differently) the game, the contest, the role, the grand prize; you are still exactly where you should be. If you want to change the outcome, then change your process and set your sights on your next life goal. No matter how large or small or what others might think. There is no goal more deserving, more lofty, substantial, or significant than your own.

Often, it's the search, not the discovery that quenches human thirst. The answers may never come. You'll not solve all of life's great mysteries. The answers you do uncover are your answers alone, for only you'll know what those little gems mean to you. When you're on your path, there's no trail leading to right or wrong; to argument or dissention. They all lead to adventure.

Remember, in the blink of an eye everything *will* change. Life will not, cannot, be exactly as it was yesterday. Accept it as part of your personal evolution. What you did yesterday affects what you do today. What you do today impacts how tomorrow will begin. All those things you want to do, see, experience, achieve, and desire are there. No one can keep you from them, except you. The underlying essence—that big chunk you should always consider when making life choices is this: *Does it provide me with a richer, fuller life?*

Keep your childlike curiosity and thirst for discovery. Explore. Relish life's mysteries, anticipating each curve in the road, each corner of every intersection. Go out there and do *any*thing! No matter what you do, you're eventually going to die. Don't paint yourself the rest of the way into that unavoidable corner. Dying is going to happen. Just don't die without living.

Consider: Why are you here? There's the obvious: your vision, dreams, goals, or perhaps just looking forward to each day as it comes. But what about the simple, "Why do you exist?" What keeps you going? What keeps you awake at night or has you looking forward to each new day? In other words, *why are you living*? Figure it out. You've got a lot to do, and whatever it is you choose to do—leave your personal stamp. Try new things. See new places. Use all of your senses. If you are not in prison, don't put yourself there. Go. Do something already!

" *When you come to a fork in the road, take it.*"

~ Yogi Berra

It's all part of the adventure.

Michael

ABOUT THE AUTHOR

Michael Holbrook is an experienced, insightful author who has written professionally since 1981. During this time, his award-winning articles, features, and essays have appeared in numerous magazines, newspapers, and professional journals worldwide. An Illinois native, he currently resides In the beautiful Southwestern United States. For more info, visit www.MichaelHolbrook.net

www.ingramcontent.com/pod-product-compliance
Lightning Source LLC
LaVergne TN
LVHW041211080426
835508LV00011B/900